**Do it**

Do It the Lazy Way (10 Quick Tips)

1. Plan your site ahead of time.

2. Let an HTML editor do the work for you.

3. Borrow ideas from other sites.

4. Look at the source code of a site you like to learn how to add new features to your site.

5. Smaller graphics help your pages load faster.

*One luxurious
bubble bath*

*Access to most comfortable
chair and favorite TV show*

*One half-hour massage
(will need to recruit spouse, child, friend)*

*Time to recline and listen to a favorite cd
(or at least one song)*

cut

Do it

6. Use logos and colors to create consistency within your site.

7. Use different font styles and sizes to offset various areas of your pages.

8. Be sure to include contact information in your site.

9. Use guest books to let your visitors communicate with you.

10. Register your site with search engines so that you can attract visitors.

COUPON

COUPON

COUPON

COUPON

cut

Build a Web Site

Build
a Web
Site

Kathryn Toyer

Macmillan • USA

Macmillan Publishing books may be purchased for business or sales promotional use. For information please write: Special Markets Department, Macmillan Publishing USA, 1633 Broadway, New York, NY 10019.

International Standard Book Number: 0-02-863018-1
Library of Congress Catalog Card Number: 98-89533

00 99   8 7 6 5 4 3 2 1

Interpretation of the printing code: the rightmost number of the first series of numbers is the year of the book's printing; the rightmost number of the second series of numbers is the number of the book's printing. For example, a printing code of 99-1 shows that the first printing occurred in 1999.

Printed in the United States of America

Book Design: Madhouse Studios

You Don't Have to Feel Guilty Anymore!

IT'S O.K. TO DO IT *THE LAZY WAY*!

It seems every time we turn around, we're given more responsibility, more information to absorb, more places we need to go, and more numbers, dates, and names to remember. Both our bodies and our minds are already on overload. And we know what happens next—cleaning the house, balancing the checkbook, and cooking dinner get put off until "tomorrow" and eventually fall by the wayside.

So let's be frank—we're all starting to feel a bit guilty about the dirty laundry, stacks of ATM slips, and Chinese take-out. Just thinking about tackling those terrible tasks makes you exhausted, right? If only there were an easy, effortless way to get this stuff done! (And done right!)

There is—*The Lazy Way*! By providing the pain-free way to do something—including tons of shortcuts and time-saving tips, as well as lists of all the stuff you'll ever need to get it done efficiently—*The Lazy Way* series cuts through all of the time-wasting thought processes and laborious exercises. You'll discover the secrets of those who have figured out *The Lazy Way*. You'll get things done in half the time it takes the average person—and then you will sit back and smugly consider those poor suckers who haven't discovered *The Lazy Way* yet. With *The Lazy Way,* you'll learn how to put in minimal effort and get maximum results so you can devote your attention and energy to the pleasures in life!

THE LAZY WAY PROMISE

Everyone on *The Lazy Way* staff promises that, if you adopt *The Lazy Way* philosophy, you'll never break a sweat, you'll barely lift a finger, you won't put strain on your brain, and you'll have plenty of time to put up your feet. We guarantee you will find that these activities are no longer hardships, since you're doing them *The Lazy Way*. We also firmly support taking breaks and encourage rewarding yourself (we even offer our suggestions in each book!). With *The Lazy Way*, the only thing you'll be overwhelmed by is all of your newfound free time!

THE LAZY WAY SPECIAL FEATURES

Every book in our series features the following sidebars in the margins, all designed to save you time and aggravation down the road.

- **"Quick 'n' Painless"**—shortcuts that get the job done fast.

- **"You'll Thank Yourself Later"**—advice that saves time down the road.

- **"A Complete Waste of Time"**—warnings that spare countless headaches and squandered hours.

- **"If You're So Inclined"**—optional tips for moments of inspired added effort.

- **"The Lazy Way"**—rewards to make the task more pleasurable.

If you've either decided to give up altogether or have taken a strong interest in the subject, you'll find information on hiring outside help with "How to Get Someone Else to Do It" as well as further reading recommendations in "If You Want to Learn More, Read These." In addition, there's an only-what-you-need-to-know glossary of terms and product names ("If You Don't Know What It Means/Does, Look Here") as well as "It's Time for Your Reward"—fun and relaxing ways to treat yourself for a job well done.

With *The Lazy Way* series, you'll find that getting the job done has never been so painless!

Series Editor and Acquisitions Editor
Amy Gordon

Cover Designer
Michael Freeland

Editorial Director
Gary Krebs

Managing Editor
Robert Shuman

Developer
Laura Poole

Director of Creative Services
Michele Laseau

What's In This Book

engines, provide ways for visitors to contact you and increase the number of visitors to your site, as well as how to manage your site in the least amount of time and with the least amount of effort.

Introduction

Who has time to read a 700-plus page computer book just to find out how to accomplish anything on the Internet? Who wants to?

After a grueling day at work, the last thing you need or want is homework. Studying a computer manual and wading through all the computer jargon is reminiscent of studying for an exam.

When you get home from work, you have chores to do—pay the bills, clean the house, prepare dinner, and do the laundry. Granted all of these things beg for an excuse to do anything but them. However, they have to be done. After all your daily responsibilities are taken care of you might have an hour each evening to spend online. And that's if you have the energy.

You don't have the time or the inclination to undertake any complicated new projects. But your boss has given you a new assignment—create the company's Web presence. Or, you have a business on the side and know you could increase your profits if you had a Web site. Or, your friends have Web pages and rave about how wonderful they are.

All you want to do is build a Web site. You don't want to spend hours or days learning how to create pages. You just want to put together a Web site as quickly and easily as possible.

You've been putting this off as long as you can. The boss keeps asking you when the company site will be up. You could quit your tedious full-time job if only your side business would grow just a little more.

If there was a quick and easy way to learn how to build a site, you'd jump on it. Well, there's no need to procrastinate any longer.

WHAT'S IN THIS BOOK

Building a Web site may sound rather complicated and time consuming. If you've ever surfed the Web and looked at some of the pages that are displayed there, you wonder how you'll ever accomplish anything quite that impressive. You just don't have the time to spend hours on such a project.

Have no fear, this book is here to rescue you. You'll learn how to create an amazing Web site in no time and with little effort.

In Part One you'll learn how to select the right software to shorten the time you spend and make the job easier. You'll learn the basics of the language of the Web. Before you begin creating your site, you need a plan. Chapter Three teaches you how to set goals and plan your pages.

Part Two teaches you what elements go into making a successful site. You'll learn about content, how to attract visitors and keep them at your site, and how to use background and fonts to enhance your pages.

In Part Three you learn how to jazz up your site with graphics, tables, lists, links, video, and audio. You'll learn the do's and don'ts of using these enhancements in your pages.

Part Four teaches you how to post your site to the Web, how to list it with various search engines, and how to get more visitors to it. In addition you learn how to make sure those visitors can contact you to give you praise, criticism or feedback.

The quick and easy sidebars and tips included within the chapters provide you with shortcuts to help you get the job done fast. Some of these sidebars define terms for you. Some give you guidelines to help you create killer Web sites.

By the time you finish this book, you'll be able to whip out a Web site in no time. You'll be a master among Web masters and the envy of all your friends and co-workers!

Part 1

Ready, Set, Go!

Chapter one

Get Ready with the Right Tools

The Internet is in the news almost daily. The stories abound of events surrounding it. One of the most popular areas of the Internet is the *World Wide Web*, called the *Web* for short. It's a graphics-rich area that allows people and businesses to strut their stuff. Turn on your television and you see Web page addresses for your local news station, at the end of movie ads, and for local businesses. Everywhere you turn you see businesses advertising their Web pages on the Internet. Many of your friends and coworkers talk about their Web pages.

There must be something to this new revolution in communication. Why else would so many people and businesses be jumping on the bandwagon?

THE WONDERFUL WORLD OF THE WORLD WIDE WEB

The Internet offers you a way to express yourself. You can let your imagination and creativity loose to create any kind of presentation you want. If you want to create pages to show

off your amateur photographs, your poetry or other writing, pictures and stories about your family, your obsession with your favorite movie or singing star, the Web gives you the means to do just about anything you want. You can build a *Web site*, which is a collection of Web pages, around any theme you desire.

Before you can begin to build your Web site, you need to have a basic understanding of the Web, the Internet, and so forth.

The Internet actually came into being in the 1970s. It came about as a result of the military's perceived need for a communication medium that would connect their various operations around the country and the world. They saw a need to have a medium that would at the same time be able to continue functioning even if a part of it was destroyed or damaged by war or disaster.

The military worked in conjunction with universities to create and test this network of networks. For approximately 20 years, the Internet was the exclusive domain of these two entities.

As part of the growth and evolution of the Internet the World Wide Web was formed. Research scientists in Switzerland developed a special language that would enable them to share their research in a centrally located area of the Internet. This special language let them link their research documents to other researcher's documents.

The World Wide Web is the baby of the Internet. It is also the fastest growing area there. At about the same time the Information Act opened the Internet up to the public in 1992, a student developed a *Web Browser* that would revolutionize the World Wide Web. A Web browser is a tool that lets you view pages on the Web.

The Web is comprised of network accessible information in documents called Web pages. These pages can and do include personal pages—pages by individuals about themselves, their interests, and so on; pages on research or student pages; pages containing scientific research or documentation/information created or discovered by students or researchers; and business pages, which contain information about them such as products, services, journals, newsletters, and so on.

This new browser was called Mosaic. It enhanced the capabilities of this once text-only medium. With this new browser, Web pages were no longer limited to text only. Now graphics and sound could be added. Since this browser was developed in 1993, many more advances in Web technology have evolved and continue to evolve.

The Web is made up of several attributes. Some of these include:

- *Graphical*   Navigation based on visual guides such as icons, pictures, text, or image maps; where you click determines where you go within pages or the Web. This type of navigation is referred to as graphical user interface (GUI).

- *Multimedia*   Provides the ability to use or view audio and video presentation as well as full-color graphics.

- *Hyperlinked*   Text, icons or pictures, and so on that lead you to other text, icons, pictures, video clip

IF YOU'RE SO INCLINED

You can find the two most popular Web browsers at the following sites:

Microsoft Internet Explorer—
www.microsoft.com/ie/

Netscape Communicator—
www.netscape.com/browsers/index.html

QUICK ● PAINLESS

IF YOU'RE SO
INCLINED

files, sounds, games, or services. Hyperlinks are similar to the links you find in the help guides of most programs. When you click on one of these hyperlinks, a new document is loaded for you to view. Every document on the Web has an address. You will notice most addresses that reside on the Web start with http://. HTTP stands for Hypertext Transfer Protocol. This is the language that tells the browser what kind of file it is and where it's located on the Internet. These addresses are also referred to as URLs, which stands for Uniform Resource Locator.

■ *Dispersed*   It is everywhere versus contained in one central location. Rather than distributed or contained within the confines of magazines to a group of subscribers in a region, state or country, it is available to thousands or millions of computers all over the world. It also has an infinite capacity for information.

■ *Dynamic*   Pages are constantly changing as they are improved or upgraded.

■ *Versatile*   Provides access not only to the Web but to other resources on the Internet such as FTP, newsgroups, gopher, and so on.

■ *Multiplatform*   Browsers are designed to work with any operating system and the Web works across a variety of different platforms from PCs or Macs to Unix host systems and even LANs.

All of these coexist to make the Web work the way it does. Web browsers such as Mosaic, Netscape Navigator, and Microsoft Explorer enable you to view Web pages in all their glory. These browsers let you hop, skip, and jump around the Web because of the way pages are linked together—the language of the Web, HTML (HyperText Markup Language). HTML is made up of special formatting codes that are embedded into documents to tell the program how to format documents. HTML weaves all these pages together similar to how a spider weaves her web. This language integrates text, sound, and graphics into seamless online documents you view as Web pages.

HELP IS ON THE WAY: WEB PAGE AUTHORING TOOLS

If you really want to spend the time learning how to use all the codes and type them out each time you need them, of course, you can. But it would take you hours and it's a very tedious process.

To simplify this whole process, some very intuitive and creative programmers have developed tools to make building Web sites quick and easy. These tools are called *HTML Editors* or Web Page Authoring programs.

With these editors, most of the tags or codes are set up as toolbar icons you simply click on when you need to use a certain formatting code. Several of these editors even have templates and/or wizards to help you create your pages.

When you use these editors, you can build a Web site in no time at all. Letting a program do most of the work

IF YOU'RE SO
INCLINED

For a comparison of Web authoring tools, check out these sites:

Ziff Davis Net—
www.zdnet.com/products/
htmluser.html

Cnet Recommends—
builder.cnet.com/Authoring/
Htmleditors/ss01.html

Ziff Davis Net Text Editor Reviews—
www.zdnet.com/products/grids/
editors.html

Ziff Davis Net WYSIWYG Editor Reviews—
www.zdnet.com/products/grids/
wysiwyg.html

for you not only saves you countless hours, but also saves you the tedium of having to type the same codes over and over. In addition you cut down on the possibility of making mistakes.

There are dozens of excellent HTML Editors you can choose from. You can download most of them from the Web. Some are freeware programs and some are shareware. Freeware means what it says—you can use the program without having to pay a fee for it. Shareware programs are set up to have you share the cost of developing them. This is usually a nominal cost. The prices found on some of the programs offered on the Web range from $19.95 to $295. Most feel within the range of $20 and $50.

Of course, you can make a trip to the computer store and purchase one of the products they have available like Microsoft® FrontPage 98, Microsoft® Internet Publisher, or Netscape® Gold. These are equally excellent programs.

However, if you want to save time and a trip to the store, the Web offers some excellent alternatives. You can also find the Microsoft programs and the Netscape programs on their respective sites on the Web.

WEB PAGE EDITORS FOR THE BEGINNER

At one of the sites on the Web that offers many different Internet related programs—the Tucows site at www.tucows.com—you can find several nice editors that were developed for the beginner. Following is a list of a few of these and how they work:

IF YOU'RE SO
INCLINED

You can find these and many other HTML editors at the following software sites:

Tucows—www.tucows.com

Strouds Apps—
cws.internet.com/32menu.html

Zdnet Software—
www.zdnet.com/products/
htmluser/downloads.html

- *Internet Creator 4.03* An easy program to use that offers wizards to walk you through each step of creating your pages. It is, however, set up mainly for business-type pages. With a little tweaking you can convert those to personal pages.

- *Hot Dog Express* An easy program to use that gives you a template to work from and requires you to move blocks over and fill in dialog boxes. It lets you choose from a variety of backgrounds and view your pages as you create them. See Figure 1.1 for an example of this editor.

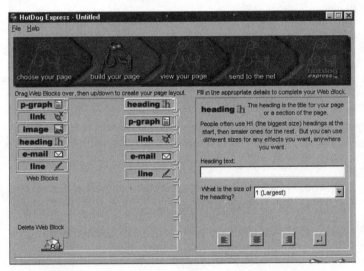

Figure 1.1 *The Setup Template for HotDog Express HTML editor.*

- *Site Builder* Offers no templates or wizards. You work directly from HTML code. It offers a toolbar with icons for the basic codes you use. However, it

QUICK **'n'** PAINLESS

HTML editors come in two varieties text editors and WYSIWYG editors. Text editors are programs that let you freely edit and create html text files. WYSIWYG stands for What You See Is What You Get. Therefore, when you use these editors, you see what you're creating as you build your site.

does have prompts to help you in designing your pages. See Figure 1.2 for an example of this editor.

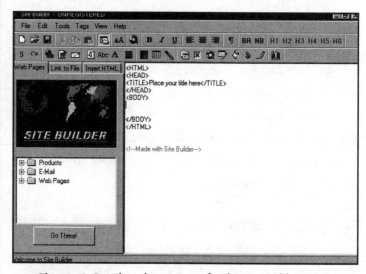

Figure 1.2   *The editing screen for the Site Builder HTML editor.*

■ *HTML Helper*   Is moderately easy to use. As with Site Builder, you work directly in HTML code on the page. However, you get no prompts, just a blank screen to work with. This program gives you a toolbar with icons along with a toolbox with the basic HTML codes as buttons you click. See Figure 1.3 for an example of this editor.

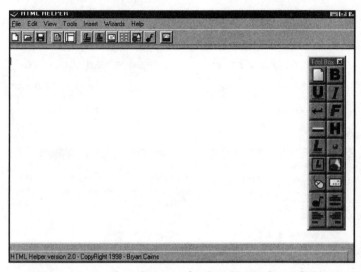

Figure 1.3   *The edit screen for the HTML Helper editor.*

EDITORS FOR THOSE WHO LIKE MORE OF A CHALLENGE

If you're one of those people who like a bit more of a challenge, there are more advanced HTML editors you can use. Whereas the beginner programs tend to walk you through many of the steps you need to take to build your site, these advanced programs assume you know enough to handle them on your own. None of them offer templates or wizards to assist you. Following are a few of these programs and how they work:

■ *1-4-All*   Of all the advanced editors, this one is fairly easy to use. You work strictly from HTML code. There are no backgrounds you can choose from. You can, however, choose a background color for your pages. To use this program, you'll need to study the

HTML codes and know when and how to use them. There are several of the basic codes as icons in the toolbar, but some of the more advanced codes are left for you to insert on your own. See Figure 1.4 for an example of this editor.

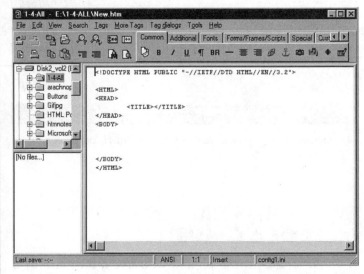

Figure 1.4 *The edit screen for the 1-4-All HTML editor.*

■ *HTML Notes* Similar to 1-4-All in that you work from HTML code with no wizards or templates to assist you. This program does give you dialogs to help you insert images, links, forms, frames, and other elements into your pages. See Figure 1.5 for an example of this editor.

■ *Arachnophilia* Has you work in HTML code to create your pages. There are no wizards or templates to help you. The basic codes are provided as icons in the toolbar that you can click on to insert. More involved codes will require your knowledge of how they work and when to use them in this program. See Figure 1.6 for an example of this editor.

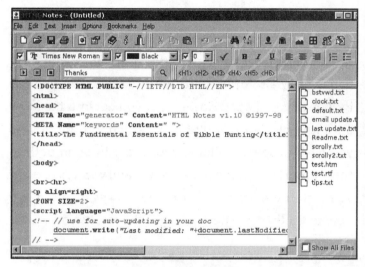

Figure 1.5 *The edit screen for the HTML Notes html editor.*

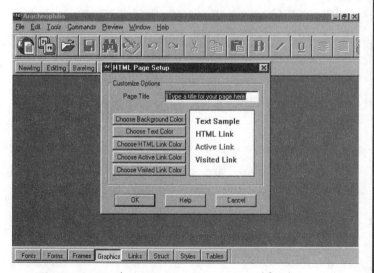

Figure 1.6 *The HTML Page Setup Wizard for the Arachnophilia html editor.*

There are many other HTML editor programs you can choose from. This is only a sampling of what's offered on the Tucows site. This should give you an idea of what's offered. You should try out a few to see which one works best for you.

Microsoft FrontPage 98 and Microsoft Publisher both offer templates and wizards to help you create your pages. They also offer more advanced elements you can include in your pages. However, as you get into the more advanced elements, you're also getting into more time you have to spend building your site. Although both of these programs offer adequate help and wizards to assist you with these advanced projects, it takes time to learn how to do them properly and get the results you want.

DON'T HANG ME UP: SERVERS AND BROWSERS

Before you can view or create these marvels of the 90s, there are a few things you need to do first. In order to view pages on the Web, you need what is called a Web browser. A browser interprets the language of the Net and converts all the codes so that what you see is beautiful pages.

There are several browsers you can use. The two most popular, however, are designed by Microsoft and Netscape. Microsoft has several versions of its browser it calls Internet Explorer. Netscape has several versions ranging from Netscape Navigator and Netscape Communicator.

As the Net grows and the Web constantly changes, these two developers are continually improving their products to keep up with the change, growth, and demand of this medium.

You need a browser not only to view other pages, but to view your pages when you finish creating them. It is advisable to get at least the browsers from these two developers so that you can be sure your pages look the way you want them to no matter what browser your visitors might use. After you create your Web pages and have them the way you want them to look, you want to make them available for others to see. You want to put them up on the Web, or *hang* them, as the Internet lingo says.

In order to hang your Web pages, you need a Web server. You may already have your own server as part of your business and your Internet presence. However, if you don't have your own server and have no desire to acquire and maintain one, all is not lost. You do have another option.

Having your own Web server is not absolutely necessary. All you really need is a program that responds to requests from Web clients. This special program is part of the service your provider includes for you. The job of this program is to make files available to users who request them through their Web browsers. An Internet connection with a service provider and a SLIP/PPP account accomplishes the same thing for you. SLIP stands for Serial Line Internet Protocol. This type of connection is a program that connects your computer to the Internet.

YOU'LL THANK YOURSELF LATER

Do a little research to discover what Internet service providers offer, what Web hosting services offer, and what is involved with being your own server. Armed with all the facts, you'll be better able to choose the best method to hang your pages on the Web.

PPP is Point-to-Point connection. It connects desktop computers to the Internet and becomes the host.

Because you want people to be able to view your site whenever they want, choosing a server or provider is very important. You want to be sure the server is reliable and its downtime is non-existent or minimal at best.

Another consideration to keep in mind is how much space you'll need. Most providers give you 1 *Meg* (megabyte) of space on their server as part of their service offering to you. Some go as high as 5 Megs. Some allow any type of page at no extra cost, while others charge separate fees to host business-related sites.

Here are some questions to ask a Web hosting provider or your ISP (Internet Service Provider) before contracting with them:

- Does the provider have its own Web server?
- How much disk space do they provide as part of their contract?
- How much does extra space cost?
- What, if any, are their restrictions regarding the type of material you can post on their server?
- Is there an extra charge for FTP space?
- Is their server online 24 hours per day?
- Is there a setup fee and if so how much is it?
- Are there monthly or usage fees?
- Can I register my own domain name and host the account there?

- Do they offer domain name registration and if so, how much is the fee?
- Can I get statistics on the number of hits to my site?
- What type support do they offer?

These questions should give you a good basis to evaluate what a provider offers and help you make the right decision in choosing a Web hosting server. You can, of course, choose to set up your own server. There are several fine server programs you can choose from. Setting yourself up as your own Web server is a very involved process. It would require a book in itself to explain all the intricacies involved. Therefore, this subject will not be covered in detail in this book. However, you can find resources to assist you in Part V.

However, bear in mind this might not be cost effective or feasible for you. In order to set up your own server, you need to have a full-time computer and Internet connection. You are also responsible for any and all problems. Unless you're a computer guru and have lots of time on your hands, it might be more trouble than it's worth. If you have a connection through a local, regional, or national provider, it's often best to let them be your host server, or to contract with an independent Web hosting provider.

Now that you know a little more about the Web and how it works, you're almost ready to start creating pages. First, you need to get an HTML editor so that you don't have to spend tedious hours creating your pages.

Then you need to make sure you have either a server or server space with a provider.

Let's move on and learn the language so you can understand what you're doing as you're creating your pages. Every page that appears on the Web is designed using the HTML language. Whether you manually use this language or depend on an HTML editor to insert it for you, it's important to have an understanding of how it works to create the final output of the pages you see.

Get Set to Understand the Language

The Web is made up of documents that are comprised of text, graphics, sounds, and other special features. All these special features and elements are woven together to create the amazing pages that you see when you surf the Web.

Each area of the Internet (such as FTP, gopher, and the Web) functions in its own specific way. Each area has its own particular language that enables users to interact with the area no matter what type of computer they use. This is a special computer language that causes each of these areas to be compatible. The Web has its own unique computer language, HTML.

You're probably wondering why you need to learn this special language. After all, the HTML editors automatically handle all this for you. True, but what if something goes wrong? Knowing at least the basics will not only help you understand how Web pages are created, but also help you troubleshoot any problems when it comes time to post your site on the Web.

TALK THE TALK: THE LANGUAGE

HTML—HyperText Markup Language—is the language of the World Wide Web. All pages on the Web are creating using the HTML language. This HTML language is made of *formatting codes* that let you set your pages up to look the way you want them to.

These formatting codes let you tell the program what size to make the fonts for headings and subheadings or titles. You can also format for special characteristics such as bold, underline, and italic. With HTML, you can add graphics and sound or video to your pages. Images can be offset or you can wrap text around them by using the correct HTML codes.

Using the right codes, you can also include background colors or images. They also let you set up lists and links to other areas in your pages or to other pages on the Web.

Without this special format coding, you would only get to create boring straight-text documents. With it, you get to create full-color pages with varying sizes of type, typefaces, pages with images in them, sound, or videos. Although many HTML editors do the coding for you, it is important for you to have a basic understanding of these codes. Understanding HTML formatting codes helps you detect when something doesn't look right in your pages and what might be the cause. This understanding helps you learn how these codes work to create your final product. These basic formatting codes for setting up Web pages are called *tags*.

YOU'LL THANK YOURSELF LATER

There are special formatting tags for every element you use to build your Web site. Learn the codes for these elements and you'll save yourself many frustrations while creating your pages as well as while managing them.

TAGS FOR EVERY EVENT

Tags come in two forms—paired and unpaired. With *paired tags*, it takes two tags to complete the formatting. You have the opening tag to tell the program to begin the format and the closing tag to tell the program to end the format. The opening tag precedes the text or word you want to format, while the closing tag is placed at the end of what you want formatted.

Unpaired tags are just that—one tag. Alone, a tag tells the program how to format anything that follows it.

Following are basic HTML tags and an explanation of what each one does.

PAIRED TAGS

- **Bold**   This bolds any text that appears between the tags. The text would look something like this with the codes revealed: <B>Sample Text</B> appears as **Sample Text** on your page when it's viewed by a Web browser.

- *Italic*   Italicizes anything between the tags: <I>Sample Text</I> appears as <i>*Sample Text*</i> in a Web page.

- <u>Underline</u>   </U> or </Underline> Underlines anything within the tags: <U>Sample Text</U> appears as <u>Sample Text</u>.

- <TITLE>Title</TITLE>   Indicates this is a title and does not appear on the page. However, it is viewed and appears in searches by Web search engines, <TITLE>The Language of the Web</TITLE>. This title

also appears in the title bar of your page, the bar at the top of the screen, when it displays in the browser.

■ <HEAD>Head</HEAD> Indicates a heading or sub-heading: <HEAD>TAGS</HEAD> appears as TAGS. Headers are broken down into six sub-categories and tagged in paired tags as <H1> </H1>, <H2> </H2>, <H3> </H3>, <H4> </H4>, <H5> </H5>, or <H6> </H6>. Each one of these tags tells the program to use a different font size, each one decreasing in size from H1 through H6.

■ <BODY> Body </BODY> Indicates a body of text.

See Figure 2.1 for an example of these paired tags in code, and Figure 2.2 for how the page looks.

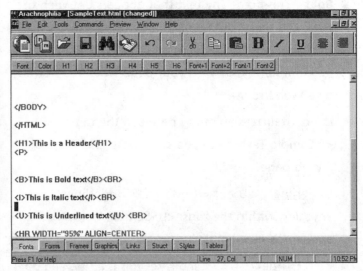

Figure 2.1 *The source code for a Web page.*

Figure 2.2 *Example showing how the code makes the page look in a Web browser.*

There are several more paired tags you can use to add formatting or various elements to your pages. The ones listed here are the basic tags. You'll use these most often. In subsequent chapters you'll learn about these other tags as you learn about other elements.

UNPAIRED TAGS

- ▪ <P> Paragraph Break, tells the program when to start a paragraph.

- ▪
 Line Break, indicates where to insert line breaks.

- ▪ <HR> Horizontal Rule, inserts a horizontal rule or line separating text or graphics and breaking up your text to make for more eye-appealing pages.

These are a few of the unpaired tags that add basic formatting to your pages and liven up your text.

You can combine any of these tags to get multiple effects, such as bold and italicized words or a bold header. Simply combine these tags like this: <B><I>Word

YOU'LL THANK YOURSELF LATER

Although not absolutely necessary, place line breaks <BR> at the end of text and paragraph tags <P> on lines of their own. This makes it easier to locate these tags and make corrections if something goes wrong.

</B></I> or <B><H1>Header</B></H1>. Just don't forget the closing tag for these paired tags.

FORMATTING WITH HTML EDITORS

All of the formatting tags and codes are handled automatically by most of the HTML editors. They are performed with a simple click on a button or menu item choice. Many of them are the same choices you would make in your typical word processing program.

For instance, the formatting for bold, underline, and italic are programmed into the B, U, I buttons in the toolbar at the top of your editor window. Centered, right-justified, and left-justified are also button selections from the toolbar, just as they are in your word processor program.

Editors make it easy for you to format your pages by keeping many of the formatting options familiar to you and what you use in your day-to-day applications. However, several of these editors require that you work in HTML code as you're creating your pages. Therefore, learning the tags will help you understand what you are doing as you're building your site. See Figure 2.3 for an example of how an HTML editor offers these tags for you. These editors automatically insert the tags for you. You simply click on the formatting code icon you wish to use.

Some of the editors include the title tag and some don't. The editors that offer the title option either include the tag with a prompt to enter your title, or offer it at the beginning of its wizards or templates. See Figure 2.4 for an example of the title tag in an editor's wizard. The tags are automatically placed there for you. You simply type in

the title you want to use. This particular editor asks for the organization or site name you want to use. This information is then inserted in the title area of the page.

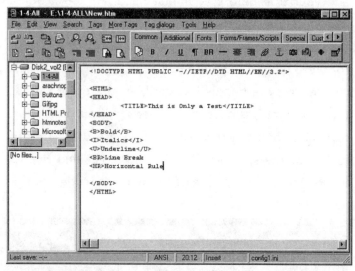

Figure 2.3 *Edit screen for the 1-4-All HTML editor showing tags inserted and tag icons in toolbar.*

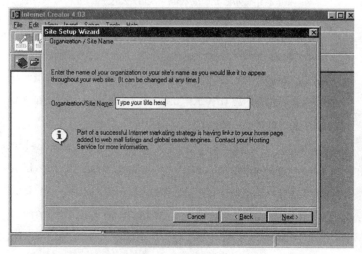

Figure 2.4 *The Site Setup Wizard for Internet Creator 4.0 showing how you enter the title information.*

Place tags in logical places. This makes the document easier to edit and work with later when you have to add information or modify the content.

If the editor you choose doesn't offer the title tag, you can add it to your pages manually. Simply type <TITLE>your title here</TITLE>. You can place this tag and your title before your first head. Placing it at the beginning of your document ensures browsers and search engines see it first and also ensures that you don't forget to place it in your pages.

Headers are handled as easily as the other formatting. You simply choose the header style you want to use from the toolbar icons. These icons are usually represented by the symbols H1, H2, H3, H4, H5, and H6. See Figure 2.5 for an example of these header code icons.

Figure 2.5 *Tool and Menu bar for the HTML Notes HTML editor showing the header code icons.*

Body and paragraph formatting are formatted automatically by editors as you type and press your return or enter key. The body of your page is formatted within the page, template, or wizard the editor offers.

To insert line breaks or horizontal rules, you select the item you want to use from the toolbar icons. Line break is represented by the symbol BR, while an icon showing a shadow line across a page or the HR symbol usually represents the horizontal rule. Depending on which of these two options you choose, the appropriate line or break is inserted. The horizontal line appears as an indented or shadow line on your page.

When you use an HTML editor, you can combine formatting simply by clicking on the formatting tools you want in the toolbar of the program you're using. It's that easy!

Any of the format codes covered in this chapter and in the following chapters can also be added to your pages manually. Simply type the tags as explained and insert the text, between the tags, you wish to appear in your pages.

If you prefer, you can also type these tags and your text into a document in your word processor. Then save the file as text only. Next, open your browser and open the file to see how the code affects how the page is viewed on the Web.

PROJECT

Of course, the quickest and easiest way to add these basic elements to your pages is to use an HTML editor. These are all elements you'll use most often when building your pages.

Let's try our hand at a few of these basic formatting tags. Don't be nervous: It's really very easy. Just follow these simple steps:

1. Open your editor and start a new document. For the purpose of the illustrations here, I am using the Site Builder HTML editor. In this particular editor, the <HTML>, <HEAD>, <TITLE>, and <BODY> tags are automatically inserted by the program. The <HTML>,

<HEAD>, and <BODY> tags are generally included in all new pages. Some of the editors also include the <TITLE> tags. All other tags you must insert yourself, either manually or by using the tag icons provided by the editor.

2. Next, let's create a title for our page. We'll use "This Is Only a Test" for our title. To create this title, type your title between the <TITLE> tags within the editor's page. If the editor you choose doesn't offer the title tag, you can enter it manually by typing <TITLE>This Is Only a Test</TITLE>.

3. After we have our title, we need the first header. Select the header type you want from the toolbar. Then type your header text, "First Test Header".

4. Next, you need a few paragraphs of text. Begin this text after the <BODY> tag and precede each paragraph with the <P> tag. This tag is represented by the paragraph symbol in the toolbar of most editors. Type a couple of paragraphs from a magazine or book.

5. If you would like a line break between your paragraphs, you need to tell the program this. Place your cursor at the end of the paragraph and select Line Break, BR, from the toolbar.

6. When you reach the end of your last paragraph, let's add a horizontal rule to separate this text from the next header or from images. Insert a line break and press Enter to get to a blank line. Select the

Horizontal Rule tag. In Site Builder, you get a dialog box that asks you to indicate the width of the line, the size of it, and how you want the line aligned. Fill in these boxes and click on the OK button.

You've just taken the first steps in creating a Web page. Although this is just for practice, you can see that it's rather simple and quick to do. See Figure 2.6 for an example of how this project should look, and Figure 2.7 for an example of how this coding affects the way the page is viewed.

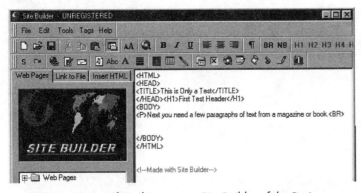

Figure 2.6 *The edit screen in Site Builder of the Project.*

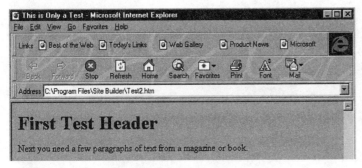

Figure 2.7 *Browser View of the Project.*

In this chapter you learned the basic formatting codes or tags you use in creating Web pages. You learned how to create them manually and how to use an HTML editor to insert them into your documents.

With these tags at your disposal, you're on your way to building your Web site. These basic codes are just the beginning! The next step is to plan your Web site.

Go! Planning Your Site

Publishing pages on the Web, simply put, is the presentation of hyperlinks in a way that gives users quick and easy access to your information. Just like with every other endeavor you undertake, to be successful, you must plan. The same holds true for your Web pages.

When planning your pages, you need to keep three issues in mind:

1. How will your pages help you reach your goal?

2. How easy will your pages be to maintain at a relatively low expense?

3. How will you measure whether your approach or specific pages are working?

REACHING YOUR GOALS

As you plan your pages, you need to set goals for them. This means you should determine the main purpose of your pages. Decide what you want your pages to accomplish. Do you want to provide information about your business to your visitors? Is advertising the main goal of your pages?

Maybe you want to use your pages for Public Relation purposes or to build your corporate image. Other excellent Web ideas are to collect contact information from visitors or to let customers order from them online. And one other excellent use of Web pages is to provide products, customer service, or technical support.

If PR is the main focus of your Web pages, you want to create pages that project a strong positive impression. Remember that almost anything you put in your Web pages makes an impression whether you want it to or not. Therefore planning is very important and what you include should be considered very carefully.

Depending on what goals you have for your site, you may not need to use all the technology that's available. For instance, if your site's goal is to provide customers with a means to order products from you, you may not need video on your site. However, if your goal is to recruit students or employees, audio, video, and other technologies will be useful in providing all the information to sway them in your favor.

The expectations of your site dictate how you design and implement your pages. Web pages can run the gamut from simple to complex.

When you outline your Web pages, they almost write themselves. Successful and effective Web pages begin with a planning outline that includes the following elements:

- *Goal or problems you want the pages to solve.*

    What you hope to gain, what problems the page

QUICK 🐭 PAINLESS

Keep it simple! The simpler the design, the more likely it is that your pages will work correctly.

will solve, and/or to disseminate or collect information, to advertise, warn, or educate.

- *Methods and materials.* What you will include: text, graphics, sound, links; where graphics or other files can be found; local sites or set up links to other sites; beta testing the site on others before you make it public.

- *Measuring success.* Collecting feedback by providing a method for visitors to respond to a set of questions or asking visitors where and how they heard about your site.

To avoid frustrating or irritating your visitors, you should plan to keep graphics to a minimum or to a size that will load quickly. Web surfers are an impatient group. If a page or graphic takes too long to come up, they will move on to other pages.

Start simple and then build. Complicated Web pages confuse visitors and could also confuse you. If you don't have a long agenda of how you want to set up your site and what you will include in that site, don't fret. Go ahead and plan something that sets up at least a simple purpose at first. You can grow and expand and even enhance your pages later on. Some elements your Web pages should contain no matter where you are in your Web authoring process include:

- *Who you are.* Which can be and should be placed at the bottom of your pages and include your email address.

- *Purpose of the site.* With a brief description of your site and its function or aim.

QUICK ⬛ PAINLESS

If you have many images, you can use thumbnails, or smaller versions, of the images to minimize download time. Then you can link these thumbnails to the larger images.

■ *Substance of your presentation.* All the content you want to include in your pages or as much of it as you are ready to present.

When creating your pages you also want to tell your visitors at the beginning the purpose of your pages. You can do this easily by concise organization and using clear, accurate headings with informative descriptions. All this should be mapped out in your planning stages.

Therefore, in planning your Web presence, keep in mind the main purpose of your presence—PR, advertising/marketing, information source, or support, technical or otherwise, for your visitors or customers. Then, plan the content of your pages—text, graphics, sound, and/or video. When planning your content, plan for how it impacts or impresses your visitors. It's always a good idea to incorporate familiar logos, mottoes, and graphics in your Web pages. This keeps you readily identifiable to your customers. See Figures 3.1 and 3.2 for examples of the FedEx and MCI pages. Notice that in these two pages the companies' logos are distinctively displayed. Also note how the graphics tie into each company's ad campaigns and general purpose.

Before you start building your site, it's wise to plan the site first on paper. One method that works quite well is a *storyboard* method. With this method you create a page with squares marked off for each page in your site. Then you fill in a rough sketch of what goes in each page in the appropriate box. These storyboards are a great way to get a clear picture of what goes where and what you need before you need it. They help you maintain design consistency throughout all your pages.

Figure 3.1 *The FedEx site.*

Figure 3.2 *The MCI site.*

Storyboards help you in planning your site, whether you're designing a single page or a series of pages. You should include a home page or front door that visitors see first. This home page also serves to orient them.

These storyboards help you to plan for adequate navigation from page to page. The last thing you need is for your visitors to get lost or frustrated. Either of these will cause them to leave and probably never come back.

EASE OF MAINTENANCE

When planning your pages, keep in mind how your pages will help you reach your goal and how easy they will be to maintain at the least expense to you.

Once you get your site put up on the Web, you'll need to perform regular updates. Visitors won't keep coming back to your site if it remains static. Therefore, you want to make sure your pages are easy to maintain.

For instance, too many graphics can become cumbersome to edit and keep track of broken links. If you have a lot of links on your pages, it can become quite a task checking all of them to make sure they're current and repair broken links.

After your site is on the Web for awhile, you'll probably get comments and feedback from your visitors, especially when you ask for them. You'll want to consider incorporating their suggestions as part of the maintenance of your site. The Web is constantly changing. New technology is released quite often. Some of that technology might be suited to the goals you have for your site. So you'll need to plan to keep abreast of these changes and learn how to use them to enhance your pages.

MEASURING YOUR SUCCESS

Along with maintaining your site, you'll also need to factor in how to determine if your pages or sections of your pages are meeting your goals or just taking up space. There are several ways to accomplish this. One is by placing *hit counters* on each page—programs that count the number of times a page is visited—or by adding *forms* to your page. These forms enable your visitors to give you information about themselves or to order from you. And you can use that information to gauge how many visitors have come to your site.

Then you need to decide how you will design your pages.

PAPER VERSUS WEB PAGES

Web pages are not linear like book pages. On the Web, you can have varying sizes of pages all intermingled together. You can have 8.5" × 11" pages mixed in with 3" × 5" pages or any size you want to make them. Basically, you can have short, fat, skinny, long, or anywhere in between in Web pages.

Then Web pages are broken up into sections. The top section is the Document Title. Following that is the content section.

In the document title section, you type a header, which is a concise name for your page. This area does not display on the page but is seen by search engines when they are searching for keywords. This document title section is also known as the window title. In Windows applications, it appears in the blue bar at the top of your window just like your filenames appear there when you open documents.

QUICK ⬤ PAINLESS

Keep in mind that Web page sizes aren't totally controlled by the person creating the pages. They're set by the viewer or browser the visitor is using. A page to a visitor is what fits within the browser window. An actual Web page can be several screens long.

A relatively new innovation for Web pages is a technique called *frames*. Frames are a more sophisticated type of coding that lets you create independent sections of a page. In essence, you're framing off these sections which work as mini-windows independent of each other.

The next section is your content area. This is where you create your actual pages and include your text, graphics, sounds, video, and so on. See Figure 3.3 for an example of a Web page with text, graphics, and video. The video isn't viewed immediately when the visitor arrives at the site. You must click on the Video or Camera icon to view it. You'll also need a separate utility in order to see the video. More about video is covered in Chapter 11.

Figure 3.3 *Example of a page that offers video.*

Text includes information you want to convey to your visitors. To make it easier for your visitors, you want to break up large pieces of text into sections. Separating these sections with lines, or horizontal rules as they are called on the Web, works nicely. Using graphics and wrapping text around them also makes for an eye-catching presentation. Another technique you can use is to insert an extra paragraph space.

The body of your pages or the content section is where you can let your imagination run wild. Use your creativity or the creativity of a friend. If you are doing this for your company call upon the creativity of your ad department to design pages that will draw visitors in and keep them there long enough to benefit from your offering.

When you think you've finished building your site, have several people look it over and give you feedback. Often, an objective third party can detect problems or errors that escape your eyes. This feedback can be an invaluable and important tool in creating an effective Web site the first time.

Web pages are written in HTML language (see Chapter 2). HTML documents break down into several parts:

- *Title.* The title of the document or the document name as discussed previously.

- *Body.* The body or content area.

- *Headings.* Major document divisions, such as headings and subheadings.

- *Paragraphs.* Body text.

- *Links.* Pointers to other parts of your document or to other documents on the Web.

Chapter 2 explained all the different HTML codes and how you use them to format your pages.

SERVERS AND BROWSERS

Once you create your Web pages and have them the way you want them to look, you want to make them available for others to see. You want to put them up on the Web, or "hang" them as the Internet lingo says.

In order to hang your Web pages, you need space on a Web server. You may already have your own server as part of your business and your Internet presence. However, if you do not have your own server and have no desire to acquire and maintain one, all is not lost. You do have another option.

Having your own Web server is not absolutely necessary. All you really need is an Internet connection with a service provider and a SLIP/PPP account. Slip and PPP are protocol languages that allow networked computers to talk to each other. Your provider has a special program called a Web server that responds to requests from Web browsers.

If you were to be your own Web server, you'd have to have a phone line and computer connected to the Internet 24 hours a day. People would then browse to you through that connection. Your provider already has the program and the 24-hour connection.

In addition to acting as the Web server, most commercial ISPs give their customers a certain amount of Web space as part of their account. You can hang your pages in that space. Ideally, this is the better route to take because the ISP's Web server is bigger, faster, and available around the clock. Plus they're responsible for the maintenance and upkeep of it, not to mention the initial investment.

A Web browser is also what you use to make sure your pages come out looking the way you want them to before you hang them. They also let you view other personal and business Web pages. You may even want to have a couple of different Web browsers on hand so that you can see what your pages look like on each of them.

Now that you have a basic understanding of what Web page authoring is and how to plan and design your pages, let's move on and learn some quick and easy ways to create an attractive, professional Web presence.

Rather than tie up your resources around the clock, use an ISP's or Web hosting provider's resources. There's really no pressing need to dedicate a phone line, a computer, the Web server software, and your time when there are companies that provide this service at a nominal cost.

The Lazy Way

Part 2

Easy as ABC

Content: The Big Easy

As you are planning your Web pages, you want to be aware of a few things. First and always, you need to keep in mind who will be visiting your site. Second, you need to be aware of what you can include in your Web site. This includes content and the technology to make your pages exciting. Knowing these elements helps you decide how you want to make your presentation.

Venturing into the world of building a Web site can seem intimidating and overwhelming. If you're not careful, you can lose sight of your goal or your audience.

Developing the content of your site is the single most important endeavor you can undertake. You need to keep your audience in mind while you're building your site. Then you need to make sure that the different sections of your site and pages benefit your site and your visitors. Lastly, you need to know when and how to link to other pages or sites. All this needs to be done while also creating manageable pages.

MEMORIES: GOALS AND AUDIENCE

While you're building your site, remember your goal. Is your goal to provide information, entertain, educate, or is it business related? With your goal in mind and as you're building your site, you want to make it noticeable, manageable, and useful.

To make your site noticeable, you want to grab the attention of visitors. There are millions of pages on the Web. In order not to be just another face in the crowd, you want to make your site as exciting, creative, and enjoyable as possible. See Figure 4.1 for an example of a site that meets these three criteria. This site uses graphics, frames, and links to make it exciting, creative, and enjoyable.

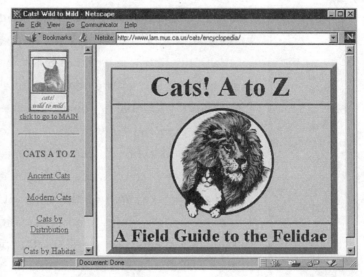

Figure 4.1   The Cats! Wild to Mild site.

Keeping your site manageable is probably the easiest as long as you don't lose yourself in creating your site. You want visitors to be able to handle and navigate it no matter which browser they use or their connection speed. Manageable means the site downloads quickly, it's set up logically so the visitor doesn't get lost or confused, and is easy to navigate.

The usefulness or entertainment value of your site is solely dependent upon you. But they are each important aspects to draw visitors to you and keep them with you.

While you're remembering your goal, also keep your audience forever in your plans. You need to consider whom it is you're trying to attract to your site.

When building your site, you'll want to include elements that are of interest to that audience. For instance, if you're creating a site about antiques, you'll want to include useful and informative text, images of antiques for illustrations, and links to related sites and/or newsgroups. Figure 4.2 is a site that includes all the elements of interest to its visitors. This site has graphics related to the purpose of the business, informative content, and links to additional information. It includes tips for home maintenance, a location map so visitors can find a store near them, and specials of the week.

Along with these elements of interest, you also want to grab your visitor's attention. This is one of the first things you want your site to do.

QUICK ☞ PAINLESS

Evaluate the various elements you can include in your pages for ease of use and your ability to learn and implement the technology, if any, involved in using them on your site.

Figure 4.2 Ace Hardware site.

WHAT'S IN A NAME: TITLES

The title for your site or pages is the first place you can get your audience's attention. This title appears in the title bar of your pages and is the first thing seen by search engines. It's also the first thing a visitor sees as the page is loading.

Choosing the right title for your pages is the first important step to take. You want a title that's descriptive and informative. You want the title to let visitors and search engines know what to expect from your site.

What do these titles tell you?

- Joe's Place

- Victoria's Palace

- Jim's Abode

- Carol's Closet

They tell you the name of the owner of the site, but not much else. You have no idea what you might find once you get to these sites.

However, with a little imagination, you can create an informative and descriptive title. Just remember how titles are used and that many visitors base their decision about which sites to visit on the title alone. Think of the purpose of your site, use the heading from your main page, or some descriptive words.

For instance, Joe's Place could become Joe's Place for Rare Antique and Collectable Cars. Victoria's Palace could become Victoria's Palace of Exotic Cats and Breeding Information. Jim's Abode could become Jim's Abode of 50s' and 60s' Music and Trivia. Carol's Closet could become Carol's Closet Packed with Short Stories, Poetry, and Artwork by Carol.

See how much more informative these titles are versus the others? Now a visitor has a better idea of what he/she can expect when he/she visits any of these sites.

DOWNSIZING: MANAGEABLE PAGES

In order to keep your audience at your site, you must make navigating the site manageable. Many people make the fatal mistake of using too many or too large graphics. Another common mistake that's made is bunching so much text together that visitors have a hard time finding what they're looking for. What you want to do is find a happy medium between providing information and entertaining. See Figure 4.3 for an example of a page that is hard to navigate because it is confusing to

QUICK  PAINLESS

Before you begin creating your site, visit several random sites. Pay close attention to their titles to get ideas about how to utilize titles to your advantage.

YOU'LL THANK YOURSELF LATER

Keep in mind that titles are the first thing search engines look at. They could very well be the only things that draw visitors to your site. A good title can draw more visitors.

the visitor, which makes it hard to navigate. The butter-fly seems to serve no purpose. The pop-up window is annoying and hard to read with its black-on-red color scheme.

Figure 4.3 *Saturn site as an example of what not to do when building your site.*

Seven Deadly Sins to Avoid in Building Your Site

1. Avoid using frames. Many people think frames are the answer to Web site navigation problems. However, frames generally cause more problems than they solve. Your visitors can't bookmark a page that uses frames, nor can you track where they are going.

2. Don't use your site as a showcase for the newest Web technology. Remember, not every visitor to

your site has the ability or the computer to support all the new technology. If she gets frustrated, you'll lose her forever.

3. Avoid complex URLs. Long URLs stand a better chance of a mistype of the address when the visitor has to type it himself. Making it short cuts down on that risk.

4. Avoid creating a haphazard or disorganized site. Many times sites are created with no clear sense of how all the components work together. This only leads to frustrated visitors to your site.

5. Avoid nonstandard link colors. One thing a visitor thinks he can count on is that links he hasn't yet seen appear in blue, while links to previously viewed pages are purple or red. Changing this color may risk confusing your visitors.

6. Remove outdated information. One of the most appealing aspects of the Web is that the information on it can change rapidly and sometimes dynamically. Keeping your site updated is one of the best ways to keep your visitors coming back.

7. Avoid long load times. I can't emphasize this enough. Any page that takes longer than 30 seconds to load stands a greater chance of losing the visitor.

One technique to consider is setting up your design so that blocks of information, graphics, and text fit on a single screen. When visitors have to scroll through many screens, it makes it more difficult to get a clear idea of all you have to offer and where to find it. See Figure 4.4 for an example of a single screen of information with links to other screens.

Figure 4.4 *Salon Magazine site with easy-to-use navigation and links to other screens.*

The idea is to present your information in an organized way that helps visitors get to their particular needs or interests easily and quickly. Headers are also a good way to introduce information to your visitors and make it easier for them to find what they're looking for. See Figure 4.5 for an example of how headers make navigating a site easier. You can use them to link to parts of the document that appear farther down.

Figure 4.5 *Example of headers in a page.*

LEADER OF THE PACK: WHEN TO LINK

Knowing when to use links is essential to successful Web pages. You can overdo or underdo links. There are several reasons to include links in your site. They are as follows:

- *Reference.*   To lead your audience to collaborating information on other sites. When you provide reference links for your visitors, you're giving them added benefits for visiting your site by giving them more of what they're looking for.

- *Related Resources.*   To lead users to other sources of information related to your site. This also helps you reduce the risk of plagiarizing. Rather than copy or paraphrase someone else's material, you can simply link to it, giving them credit.

- *Organization.* To reduce clutter by linking to other areas in your site. Rather than have one overly large page packed with a lot of information that can seem overwhelming to a visitor, you can create several pages and provide links within text or images to the other pages. See Figure 4.6 for an example of a page with useful links.

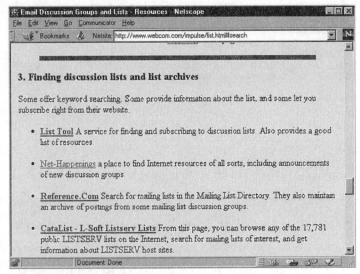

Figure 4.6 *Page with useful links.*

Just as there are reasons to link, there are reasons *not* to link. One of the main reasons not to link to another site could be offensive material. Be aware of young visitors and the potential for problems there. Also you don't want to drive visitors away by linking to these types of sites. Unless, of course, you're creating this type of site and want to attract visitors who enjoy that type of material. In that case, you should warn your audience of the type of material on your site.

Anytime you have links to material that could be considered offensive, you need to be sure your visitors know where those links lead and the type of material they'll find once they get there. See Figure 4.7 for an example of a page with links to offensive sites with warnings to the visitors.

Figure 4.7 *Page with links to objectionable material and warning.*

The next reason not to link to a site is if it is a large directory listing of FTP sites. Many people who have access to the Web have programs that can't handle these large directories. Also, if you only need to link to one or two files within that directory, you're wasting your visitors' time by having them search through these large

TEN RULES FOR GOOD WEB PAGE DESIGN

1. **Use descriptive and informative titles.**

2. **Create your pages for easy viewing on any browser.**

3. **Use logical formatting.**

4. **Sign and date your pages.**

5. **Provide text alternative to graphics.**

6. **Put links into context.**

7. **Keep heading levels small, logical, and consistent.**

8. **Test your site's presentation on several browsers.**

9. **Keep graphics small.**

10. **Provide text alternatives to frames.**

directories of files. Simply link directly to the files that are pertinent.

WHAT YOU CAN INCLUDE IN YOUR PAGES

The sky's the limit when it comes to what you can use to build your Web site. The Web is the most versatile of all the mediums on the Internet. It's not limited to text only, such as the other services of email, newsgroups, and chat.

Following are some of the elements you can use to build an effective, informative, and impressive Web site:

- Text
- Local Links
- Graphics and Clip Art
- Sounds
- Video and Animation
- Forms
- Frames
- Links to Other Sites and/or FTP Sites
- Scripts
- Contact Information
- Bulleted or Numbered Lists
- Tables
- Downloadable PDF Files

TEXT

Text is the number one element you want to include in your Web site. Without it, you would be hard pressed to convey essential information. Even sites that have mostly links use text to establish those links and explain what they are.

Too much text can be as much of a problem as too little. Use it wisely and succinctly. And when you use text, use headings so readers can quickly zoom into topics that are of interest to them. See Figure 4.8 for an example of a page with text presented in an organized manner.

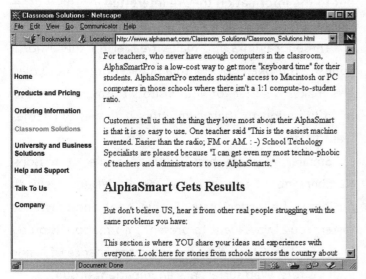

Figure 4.8 *AlphaSmart page which shows good topic headers and content organization.*

Be aware that not everyone in your audience has graphics capabilities. You may also have visitors who are sight impaired. To make sure anyone can get the most benefit from your site, you can use text as an alternative to your graphics. Pictures can make a very pleasing site to look at, but they're worthless if the viewer can't see them.

LOCAL LINKS

Links in Web pages come in two varieties—local links and links to other sites or Web pages. Local links are links to other pages or areas within your site. Links to other sites or Web pages are just what it says—links to sites or pages other than your own.

Using links to other parts or pages in your documents makes it much easier for visitors to navigate your site and get to the information they're interested in. This is especially useful if you have a large site.

These local links also make it easier for the visitor if your site is broken down into a number of separate files. This makes it easier for your visitors to save smaller bits of information to their computers if that is what they want to do.

Smaller files are better for a couple of reasons. Number one, of course, is they are easier and faster to navigate. The second reason is they open and download faster. You always want to present information as quickly as possible. Otherwise, you stand the chance of losing your visitors. Web surfers are an impatient group.

GRAPHICS AND CLIP ART

Graphics and artwork is what jazzes up your site. It's what makes it pleasing to the eye of your visitors and makes them want to see more or stay at your site. A site with only text becomes boring to the eyes very quickly. Therefore, you want to use some kind of graphics to break up text and keep your visitors interested in exploring your site.

However, you don't want to overdo it with graphics and you want to be careful not to use extremely high resolution graphics or large graphics files. The longer it takes your page to load, the more chance there is your visitor will leave your site to surf elsewhere.

You can use any format you want in your Web pages; however, the standard is either the GIF or JPEG format (see Chapter 9 for more information). These two are compressed graphics formats and tend to be smaller files. See Figure 4.9 for an example of a page with good use of graphics. It adds value to the shopping and searching experience of its visitors. It provides side-by-side photos and descriptions of a category of products. It's almost like going to the store and physically comparing the products next to each other.

IF YOU'RE SO
INCLINED

Following are a few sites where you can get graphics to use on your pages:

Artlinx—
desktoppublishing.com/
artlinx.html

Free Stuff made available by desktopPublishing—
desktoppublishing.com/
freestuff.html

Top Ten Clipart Collection—
www.pcworld.com/news/daily/
data/0198/980130113237.html?
SRC=watch

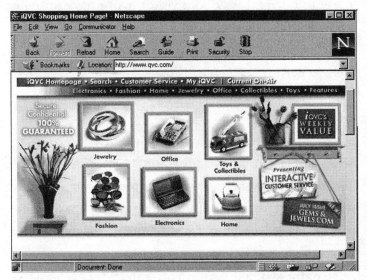

Figure 4.9 *QVC Shopping Home Page showing use of graphics to link to various areas of the site and tie in with company's goal.*

AUDIO

Sounds are another way you can attract and keep visitors at your site. You can have sounds playing in the background as the visitor is navigating through your offerings. Or you can use a sound file to welcome him.

Sounds are a good way to convey information to your visitors. This would be similar to sound bites you hear on radio or news shows. As the technology for the Web has improved so has the quality and types of sounds you can use.

Before you consider using sounds in your site, there are a few things you should be aware of. First, sounds tend to be rather large files, therefore they can take a long time to download. Second, the quality of audio files isn't always great. The technology is improving, but has a way to go yet. Lastly, your visitor might have to use a separate utility or plug-in in order to enable her to hear your audio file. Plug-ins are small programs that enable users to perform certain activities.

VIDEO

Videos are another element you might want to consider when building your Web site. Digital videos can be used to give a tour of something of interest to you and your visitors. You can convert home videos to digital video to let the world see your favorite family videos. If you attend parties with other online friends, you can tape video of these gatherings and offer them for everyone to see on your Web site.

IF YOU'RE SO INCLINED

The following are some sites where you can get audio files:

Classical Midi Archives—
www.prs.net/midi.html

GaryW0001's Midi Homepage—
garyw0001.simplenet.com/frames.html

Midi files—
www.midifiles.org/

As with audio files, there are some restrictions to using video files you should be aware of. Video files are very large files that can take a very long time to download. They can be quite expensive to compress and convert to computer files. In addition, these files often require the visitor have a plug-in or other utility in order to view. For all this trouble, visitors expect videos to be worth viewing. They should impart information in an entertaining and informative manner.

The number of ways you can use video are countless. With the increase in the capabilities of technology, most users have machines that are able to view these videos. The technology is improving all the time and the quality of these videos is getting better. See Figure 4.10 for an example of a Web site with video.

Figure 4.10 *DenTV site showing video opened.*

Animation is a technique you can use to spice up your Web site. Animation, in essence, adds movement to graphics. This can look like cartoons or like the dancing baby you see on the Ally McBeal television show.

This technique can be as useful as small snippets to show how a particular product works. It can also be used strictly for entertainment purposes.

FORMS

Forms are great for collecting information and feedback from your audience. If you have a product to see, they're an excellent way to have your customers give you feedback on what they would like to see on your site as well as information about your product's usefulness to them. See Figure 4.11 for an example of a form in a Web site.

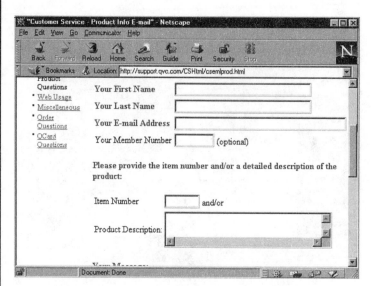

Figure 4.11 QVC Customer Service site with a customer service form.

Forms are a good way to offer your products for visitors to order. However, you need to be security conscious when enabling users to order online. There are excellent security programs you can install. There are also several services that offer to handle payments securely for you for a nominal fee.

FRAMES

One of the newest innovations in Web pages is frames. These frames let you partition off or frame sections of your pages. Then these partitioned-off sections can function independently of each other. See Figure 4.12 for an example of a Web site utilizing frames.

You can find security software and/or information at these sites:

Computer Security Information —
www.alw.nih.gov/Security/
security.html

Telstra Corporation: Computer and Network Security Reference Index—
www.telstra.com.au/info/
security.html

Netsurfer Focus: Computer and Network Security—
www.netsurf.com/nsf/v01/01/
nsf.01.01.html

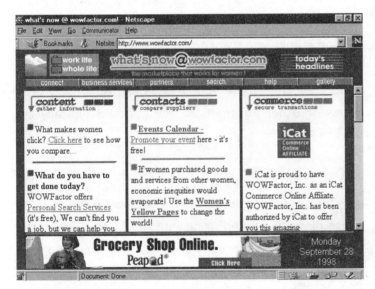

Figure 4.12 *Wow Factor Women's page with frames.*

When you use frames, it enables you to provide more information seemingly in one page, while letting visitors access links to other pages. When a user is in one of these frames, it appears the information just changes without a new page loading.

The problem with using frames is that not every Web surfer has the capability of viewing these types of pages. Therefore, if you choose to use frames, you'll need to offer alternative non-frame pages. Also, you can't bookmark a document within a site using frames, because the URL never changes.

LINKS TO OTHER PAGES OR SITES

Links are one of the things that make the Web such a wonderful place. Links let you give your visitors all the information they want without having to create it yourself. They help support your site and the information on it.

Some links you want to consider including are links to other sites or pages that would be of interest to your visitors or sites where your visitors can download programs or other information. These would typically be links to FTP sites.

DOWNLOADABLE PDF FILES

PDF files are Adobe's Portable Document Format files. These files are created using PostScript, which puts the document in formats ready to print. They require a special reader program that Adobe also makes. The reader is freeware but the page maker isn't.

The IRS is an excellent user of these PDF files. They use them to offer forms to their users. The user selects the form to open in the Adobe reader and the visitor can

QUICK 🖱 PAINLESS

Providing links to other sites and other people's pages can result in reciprocation—links back to your site. This can increase your hit count considerably.

print the form which then looks very similar to the forms he gets at the post office, library, or directly from the IRS.

Offering PDF files is an excellent way to convert your print-ready documents, forms, and so forth to the Web, thereby offering universal documents to all your visitors and customers. It gives them a sense of familiarity and professionalism.

SCRIPTS

Scripts are programs that work within your pages to perform events that enhance your site. If you have the knowledge, you can create these scripts yourself, or you can borrow them from others who have had the time and the expertise to create them.

You can use scripts on your pages for any number of activities. You might want to use a script to provide your visitors with a means to search your site for specific information. You can use scripts to set up a discussion board to let your visitors chat with each other or with people in your company. Scripts can be used to display random images on your site. There are many other ways you can use scripts, but this gives you an idea of how they can benefit your site.

Scripts come in a variety of forms. There are Java Scripts, Java Applets, CGI scripts, and ActiveX scripts. There are several places on the Web where you can find any number of these scripts. When we get to the chapter that deals with some of the more advanced Web page building techniques, we'll get into where you can find these sites.

CONTACT INFORMATION

One of the best things you can do for yourself, your site, and your visitors is to include contact information. This gives your audience a way to contact you if they experience problems. It also gives them an outlet to praise your site or give you suggestions on how to improve it.

In addition, if someone would like to link to your site or use it for reference, contact information within your site makes it much easier for them to get your permission before hand. They can also notify you when your site is going to be used.

Contact information generally means an email address of a person the visitor can contact with questions, comments, or suggestions. If someone else creates your site for you, you might also want to include his email address, such as Webmaster—webmaster@provider.com.

Be aware that including this information opens you up to receiving junk email. Many of the companies that mass email use what are called *bots,* special programs, to search Web pages for email addresses. These special bot programs gather these email addresses into a database that is used by these companies to send advertisements much like direct mail campaigns you receive through normal mail.

LISTS AND TABLES

Lists and tables are useful in presenting information in an organized form. They let you present information that lets the eyes flow through your presentation. You can use lists or tables for various types of information.

For instance, you can use lists for your Table of Contents. You can also use them for a grouping of your links. Tables can be used to present statistical or other forms of data. See Figure 4.13 for an example of a page with a Table of Contents in list format.

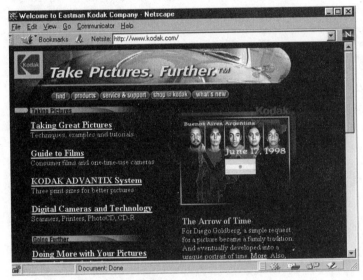

Figure 4.13 *Kodak site with Table of Contents in list format.*

Each of these elements breaks up otherwise long areas of text and gives the reader's eyes a rest. They also enhance the look of your site.

In this chapter, you learned the various elements you can use to build and exciting and entertaining Web site. Use the examples given in this chapter to give you ideas about what you can use, as well as how to organize your site in the most pleasing way. You objective is to draw visitors into your Web site and keep them there.

You also want to provide them with what they're interested in or need. Sometimes that means you lead them out of your site. However, if you've done an effective job of designing your site, they'll come back or even better yet, bookmark your site so they can come back to it another time. Next, you learn how to take all these techniques, put them together, and start building your site.

Chapter five

Looking Good

You're not considering creating a Web site to do a **haphazard job of it. Not any old site will do.**

You want a site that looks good, is exciting, and keeps visitors exploring it. This can be quite a chore if you approach it blindly.

There are several areas to concentrate on—site design, page layout and design, content, and navigation. How you use all of these not only creates an exciting and attractive site, but it also holds your visitor's interest.

IF YOU BUILD IT, WILL THEY COME?

Just because you build a site and put it on the Web is no guarantee that people will visit it or even come back once they do. If your site is hard to navigate around, disorganized, or just plain badly built, they most certainly won't return.

The Web is jam packed with sites and pages. Why would a person want to stick around, bookmark, or come back to a site that's boring, frustrating, or poorly designed? Would you? Probably not.

Therefore, it's your job to build usability and value into your site. You want to build a presence that not only looks good but also keeps your visitor hooked while meeting his or her goals.

Understanding what your visitors want also helps you determine the type of site to build. There are two basic types of sites you can build—those that provide information or educate and those that provide entertainment. Visitors to informational/educational sites want that information fast and in an easy-to-digest format. Entertainment sites draw visitors who want to see something cool and to have fun. For entertainment sites even more than informational sites, the design is as important, if not more so, than content. Game sites are prime examples of how important a part design plays in their presentation. See Figure 5.1 for an example of an entertainment site and Figure 5.2 for an example of an informational site.

With your visitors in mind, you also have to remember that visitors have a number of ways they can enter your site. They don't always come in through the front door. Visitors can come to you through search engines, bookmarks they receive from friends, and links from other pages.

No matter which door they enter through, you need to make sure they know where they are, where they can go, and what you have to offer. You want to give them a preview of what's under each level of your site without revealing all its contents; entice them to keep looking. Yahoo!'s site is an excellent example of how this is done (see Figure 5.3).

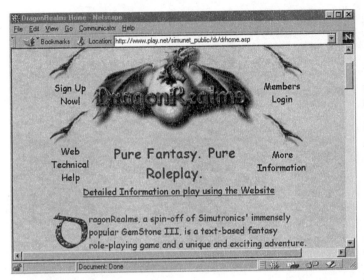

Figure 5.1 Dragon Realm game site.

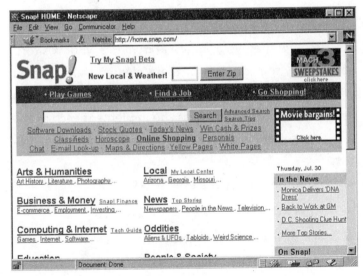

Figure 5.2 Snap Online's site.

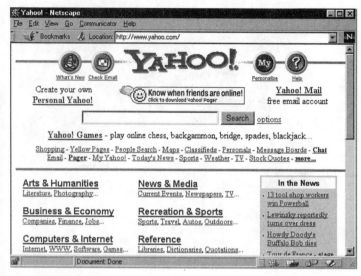

Figure 5.3 The Yahoo! site.

There are several ways you can make sure that your site accomplishes your goals and meets your visitors' needs. Only the concepts of these elements are covered in this chapter. When you're designing your site, you need to keep these in mind as you implement each of the techniques that make up a site. These concepts are as follows:

- Design the site for the user
- Always identify your site
- Make sure visitors can always find their way
- Make good use of links
- Keep your pages short and focused
- Don't use a graphic when text will do
- Design your site for the greater audience

- Design icons carefully
- Test your pages on actual users
- View other sites to get ideas

WHO GOES THERE: DESIGN YOUR SITE FOR THE USER

Many people who design sites make the mistake of designing them on how a company is structured. Rarely is that helpful to anyone who visits the site. A site's categories should be designed in terms of what the visitors want when they come to your site.

Generally this means structuring your site in a hierarchical manner. This means going from general to specific details, starting with a large category and descending through subcategories. This is much like how a book is designed. See Figure 5.4 for an example of a site that descends through subcategories to organize its material. The subcategories are much like a table of contents for a book. They let the viewer know what each topic covers. Then all the visitor has to do is pick a topic of interest, and the Web site opens to that page.

If you were designing a site for writers, you might start off with a section called Writing Techniques, which is then divided into subcategories of Short Story Writing Tips, Novel Writing Tips, and Poetry Writing Tips. Then you could break each of those sections down to specific subcategories.

For example, you don't want to put all the sections of your site on one page. What you want to do is provide

YOU'LL THANK YOURSELF LATER

Using scale to vary elements in your site also helps in establishing a hierarchy. For instance, you can use large elements to let your visitors know what the really important areas are.

the visitors with major topics that are linked to more information in the other sections. That way if a visitor clicks on Short Story Tips, she gets a page with the topics under that category. She then chooses the topics she wants to read.

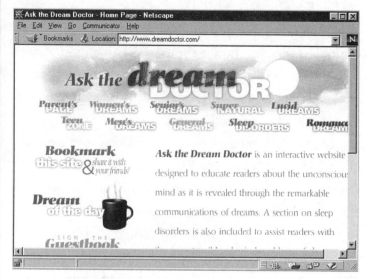

Figure 5.4 *The Dream Doctor site.*

Other than the hierarchical method, there are two other approaches you can use, depending on the type of site you're building. One is the table-driven structure and the other is the linear format. You would use the table-driven structure to organize aggregated or historical data, such as sports statistics and the like. The linear for-mat is ideal when the information you're presenting has a logical sequence to it, such as recipes or step-by-step procedures.

With the Web it's almost impossible to control how visitors will ultimately use your site. They decide how much reading they'll do, how much scrolling they're willing to do, and whether they want to see graphics. And you shouldn't want to control your visitors too much. You want them to use your site to get what they want and need out of it.

With that in mind, you can learn from your users. You can learn what they want and how to give it to them. Keep the site focused on what the visitor wants and needs and you're on your way to a successful site.

WHERE AM I? ALWAYS IDENTIFY YOUR SITE

One thing you want your readers to do when they visit your site is identify with it no matter where they come from and where they are in your site. You can accomplish this in one very important way—consistency.

You want to put your company logo and name or your site's name on every page. You can even make this logo a link to the home page of your site. This makes it easier for the visitor to get back to the beginning anytime he wants.

Another method you can use for consistency is to use the same background and color schemes for all the pages on your site. This is a simple method to establish familiarity.

Along with the identifying logo for your site, you want to make sure that your site has a set style. You'll want to have some repeated elements. This helps the

IF YOU'RE SO INCLINED

You can track how your visitors enter and wander through your site with software that logs and tracks visitors. This software is called Web site tracking programs. For instance, Web Trends Professional is an example of this type of software. Here are a couple of sites where you can find this software:

Ziff Davis Software— www.zdnet.com/products/downloads.html

Builder Downloads— www.builder.com/Downloads

QUICK ✏ PAINLESS

Placing your logo or site symbol on each page, in the same spot, and making it the same size creates consistency and a sense of comfort with your visitors.

YOU'LL THANK YOURSELF LATER

The names you choose for the sections of your site have an influence on how visitors react to those sections. They also assist in guiding them through your site. Choose your section names carefully. Think of their connotations, feelings they evoke, as well as the actual meanings.

visitor identify with you and it makes it easier for you to maintain your site. It saves you from having to rebuild an entire page from scratch each time you need to make changes.

This consistency in your site makes your visitor feel at home and gives him or her something to identify with. For example, using the same fonts, colors, logos or site symbols, and graphics on all the pages in your site lets the visitors know they're still in the same site. The consistencies of these elements are things he or she can identify with your site.

THEY WENT THAT AWAY: MAKE SURE VISITORS CAN ALWAYS FIND THEIR WAY

When you design your site, you'll likely to divide it into sections. You might even call these sections neighborhoods. You'll want to make sure your visitors can always find their way around your site. If a visitor gets lost while trying to find specific information at your site, he'll leave and probably not come back. In addition, he could tell others not to bother visiting your site.

The visitors to your site aren't passive. They have their own way of getting around your site. Therefore, as you're designing your pages, you need to keep ease of navigation in mind. The best thing you can do for your site and your visitors is to offer multiple approaches to get to the same information.

There are several ways you can do this. You can have arrows leading from page to page for visitors who want to proceed through your pages sequentially. HTML links are another way to let visitors bounce between different pages in any way that suits them. Using text links such as related links with three or more links at the bottom of a page helps visitors choose other pages they want to view.

No matter what method you choose, you need to make sure that any navigational aids are prominent in your design. Visitors want to be able to find what they're looking for and get to it quickly. See Figure 5.5 for an example of how navigational aids (such as the alphabet linked to other pages) help visitors easily find their way around this site.

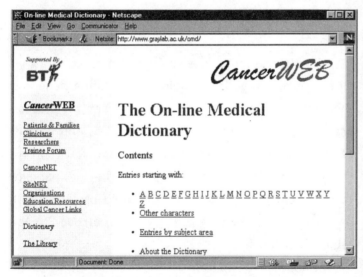

Figure 5.5 *The Online Medical Dictionary site.*

When you use icons to represent navigation, be sure to use a graphic that the visitor can easily understand.

Make these icons stand alone to describe what the visitor does or what happens when he clicks on the icon.

Another way to do this is to leave "bread crumbs" for them to follow. This involves always providing links from the home page down to the current page and then on to other pages. This approach lets the visitors find their way around your site to the information they're looking for, no matter where they are.

If you choose to use text links as navigational aids, be brief and concise. Select words that convey what the visitor can expect on the other end of the link. The link should entice the visitor to click, and the link itself should deliver what your text promises. For example, next page, back to main page, download abc software, or newsletter for teens.

Along those same lines you want to make sure that all the pages on your site point to the home page and their own parent pages. You *never* want to have an orphan page that ends in a blind alley. This only confuses your visitors. To alleviate this problem, you can provide a link back to the home page, to a previous page, or to other pages. For instance, you could provide a link back to previous page, to related links, or back to the table of contents.

Including a navigation bar is a smart thing to do when building your site. A navigation bar is a distinct area on the page that gives you options for moving around in the site. It lets visitors know what they can do at your site. Therefore, it's a good idea to make sure you have this navigation bar load first. You can do this by

QUICK PAINLESS

The bread crumbs you leave give your visitors context and lets them travel back up the hierarchy without having to go through all the intermediate points.

putting it at the top of your pages. See Figure 5.6 for an example of a page with an excellent navigation bar.

Figure 5.6 *Ace Hardware site with navigation bar.*

Another approach you can use to assist your visitors in navigating your pages is to offer a means to search your site for the information they want. No matter how well you provide navigation help for your visitors, they need to be able to search if they get lost. Giving them a search tool offers them escape routes if they do get lost. See Figure 5.7 for an example of a search tool as part of a Web site.

Be aware that the programming software required to include a search engine in your site is difficult to master if you don't have a programming background. It can also be expensive to acquire. For that reason it won't be covered in detail in this book.

A COMPLETE WASTE OF TIME

Not all sites need to have search tools. Some, in fact, are inappropriate to have these tools. Very small sites or sites with little actual data don't need to be and shouldn't have search capabilities.

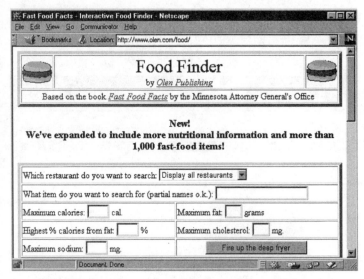

Figure 5.7   *The Fast Food Facts site with a search tool included.*

LOOSE LINKS SINK WEB SITES: MAKE GOOD USE OF LINKS

All browsers have default settings that display visited links in a different color than links the user hasn't visited yet. It's best not to alter this scheme. There are too many other ways that you can make your site distinguishable without having to fool with something most visitors are already familiar with. Remember that if visitors can't figure out where they've been and where they haven't been, they could get frustrated and leave. You certainly don't want that.

Hyperlinks play a major role in your pages. There are many ways you can handle them. Get creative in how you lay them out on a page. For instance, you can list them horizontally across a page. You can also set them up in a table format. Tables are covered in depth in Chapter 8.

Also, when using links, you want to make sure they are clear and easy for the visitor to use. Use labeled links instead of directional ones. Instead of using *back* and *up,* use section names, page titles, and other content-revealing labels on your navigational links. However, when *next* and *previous* can be understood easily, it is acceptable to use them. For instance, if you have a story that continues onto another page, the next and previous labels work fine.

The important thing is to make sure your visitors know where they're going when they click on a link. You also want to check your links periodically to make sure they are still valid and replace or delete any broken links.

YOU SNOOZE, YOU LOSE: KEEP YOUR PAGES SHORT AND FOCUSED

Rather than have one large page with several different topics of information, break them up into individual pages with a separate page to index and link them.

Keeping your pages short does a couple of things. First, Web surfers tend to be an impatient group. They don't have the time or the inclination to spend scanning through large documents for the information they want. When you're building your site, you want to make sure it loads quickly and gets your visitors involved instantly. One way to increase the speed of your site is to limit each page to between 15K and 20K for your HTML files and to between 20K and 35K for your graphic and animation files. The small file sizes load quickly for surfers with 28.8Kbps modems and like lightning for those with T1 connections. You can keep HTML file sizes small by using hyperlinks for navigation instead of graphic buttons. Some sites offer their visitors a text-only version. This text version loads faster and is user friendly for the sight-impaired.

They may be interested in one area you provide information, while having no interest whatsoever in other areas. Shorter pages with an index page give them the opportunity to choose what they want to view.

Second, shorter pages are easier for you to design as well as easier for the visitor to handle. Remember that somewhere down the line you're going to have to maintain your site. A shorter page is much easier to edit and modify than a long one.

Stay focused and you'll help your visitors stay focused. When they stay focused, they stay at your site and continue to explore what you have to offer.

WORDS ARE WORTH MORE THAN PICTURES: DON'T USE A GRAPHIC WHEN TEXT WILL DO

Remember you're not just designing this site for your own pleasure. You're designing it for your visitors. Therefore, it's unnecessary to put text labels in graphics just because you want to show off a particular font.

Designating in code the type of font and color you want to use is sufficient. If the viewer of your page wants to read your page in a font that's more comfortable for her, she'll adjust her browser to alter the fonts anyway.

YOU'LL THANK YOURSELF LATER

Making these extra graphics only slows down your page and annoys the visitor. An annoyed visitor is likely to leave and never come back.

NO BUSINESS LIKE SHOW BUSINESS: DESIGN YOUR SITE FOR THE GREATER AUDIENCE

There are many different types of visitors who can come to your site. You can't possibly build your site to please them all. However, you can design it so that you at least meet the needs of those with special needs.

There are a lot of Web surfers that aren't Generation Xers. The Baby Boomers, for instance, are getting to the age when their eyesight isn't what it used to be. Small type on a screen is almost impossible for them to read. Rather than adjust their browsers to larger font sizes, they may just leave your site.

You also need to consider the sight-impaired. You don't want to leave these people out when building your site. By including them in your audience, you're targeting an important group and you're making your pages more accessible. Many people use alternative platforms to access the Web, such as handheld devices, speech programs, and so forth.

To accommodate this audience, you need to include either text-only versions of your pages, or text alternatives. Text alternatives would be descriptions of graphics where used. For instance, as the image loads, or if the visitor chooses no graphics, text is displayed to describe the graphic, such as picture of a red box, click here for yes, or an aerial map of the city of Dallas.

The colors you use can greatly affect the readability of your site. When you make it hard for visitors to read, you run the risk of losing them forever. There are some colors that are hard on the eyes, lime green, for instance. Also there are colors that aren't particularly attractive either, such as diarrhea-brown.

SHOW DON'T TELL: DESIGN ICONS CAREFULLY

Icons are small graphics you use to convey meaning to visitors to your site. Using them is a good way to build consistency in your site. However, they need to be designed well enough that they can stand on their own.

In other words, if an icon needs a label, it's not doing its job. Work on your icons until they can stand alone and convey the meaning you intend. Otherwise, replace them with a text link or a labeled button.

Another method you can use to help your visitors get around your site is what is called a mouse-over, tool tip, or hover technique. With this technique, when the visitor places the cursor over a graphical link, a small tip or hint displays for them in the status bar. This technique is covered in Chapter 9.

This offers the visitor something they are familiar with in other applications. They are used to receiving helpful information as they wander around. Using these mouse-overs you can help them navigate around your site.

LOOK BEFORE YOU LEAP: TEST PAGES ON ACTUAL USERS

When it comes time to test your site, test it on actual users. Find people who are part of your intended audience and let them tell you how well the site is designed.

A COMPLETE WASTE OF TIME

■ Don't use a tooltip or hover technique to cover up poorly designed icons.

■ Don't label icons.

Co-workers and friends just don't give you the kind of feedback you need in order to build a successful site. Since they're not part of the target audience, they won't be aware whether your site is missing vital information you need to convey.

When you're testing your site, try to find out where visitors come from, where they go on your site, and where they go when they leave. The answers to these questions will help you understand how people actually use your site and help you design it to meet their needs.

One method to get information from your test subjects about your site is to use index cards. Give these test subjects a stack of index cards with the topics covered in your site. Have your testers sort the cards into categories. If necessary, suggest categories for them. When you get the cards back, note how they are sorted. If a topic is sorted into two different categories, you need a cross-link between those categories.

Next, test your site on all the browsers your visitors use to view Web pages. You can, of course, consciously decide not to support a certain browser or system. But do so deliberately, not by omission.

If you do choose not to support a certain browser, be sure to indicate that on your pages. In turn, if you know a certain technology you're using won't work on certain systems, be sure to say so on your site. For instance, some browsers can't display frames. The other option is to simply not use options that won't work on certain systems or browsers.

QUICK ⬤ PAINLESS

One method you could use to get feedback is to set up a test group. Then use an email survey to get responses from your testers. Set up a group list in your email program for the people in your test group. Mass mail them the survey requesting that they respond back to you within a given time frame.

Making sure your site is easily readable, easy to navigate, well organized, and exciting goes a long way in attracting visitors and keeping them there once you get them.

DON'T REINVENT THE WHEEL: VIEW OTHER SITES TO GET IDEAS

Take a look around the Web. Windows show at other sites.

As you surf the Web, pay attention to how others have designed their sites. Take notes about what you like and don't like. Bookmark your favorite sites.

While you're at these sites, use what you see to get ideas for how you want your site to look. Then take it one step further. Look at the source code to see how they created their sites. Each browser offers an option under the View menu to review a page's source code. You can then print this source code out so you have a handy reference when you build your site.

Be sure to make notes on this printed page so you don't forget why you need it later, such as code for cool table for my site, or code for great background color or wallpaper.

A FOUNDATION TO BUILD ON

Part of building your site is designing the individual pages. You want to design them so they're consistent and so that they don't confuse your visitors. And you want to do this without your pages becoming boring.

One way to keep your pages consistent without becoming monotonous is to use similar elements that change slightly from page to page. This could be a graphic that changes, such as a ball that changes color or positions on each page. It could be a picture of a person in different clothes or positions. Of course, whatever you use it is better if it relates to the focus of your site.

Another method is to use text as a design element that differentiates the various sections of your site. You can do this by changing the thickness of letters or the font style to develop a special identity for each section.

Next, while creating your pages, consider how you're going to present your text. Large bodies of text can overwhelm visitors. Especially when it's present from left-to-right and margin-to-margin. It's very hard to read and the eyes get tired quickly with the large blocks of unbroken text.

If you want to keep from scaring off your visitors, try breaking the text into columns. However, be careful when you do this. You don't want to make your visitors scroll down and then back up to read your information. You can solve this problem by making the pages smaller and splitting the text into two columns. Then continue the text onto another page with a next page link. CNET's NEWS.COM site is an excellent example of placing text in columns. See Figure 5.8 for an example of how CNET puts their information into columns on their page.

YOU'LL THANK YOURSELF LATER

Be careful when emphasizing words. Following are some general guidelines to use:

- Try not to use bold for more than a line or two of text

- Use bold when you want to shout

- Use bold only on working words within a sentence rather than words that carry no meaning

- Bold shows up better than italics in most Web pages

- Never use all caps for emphasis

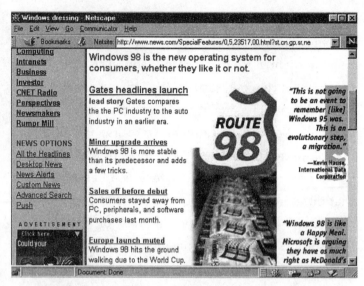

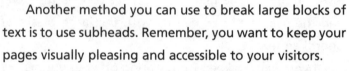

Figure 5.8 *CNET NEWS.COM site showing columns.*

Another method you can use to break large blocks of text is to use subheads. Remember, you want to keep your pages visually pleasing and accessible to your visitors.

Subheads serve two purposes. One, they give the reader's eyes a short break. And, two, they let readers scan your page to find the areas they're interested in. Of course, you can combine columns and subheads to break up text.

While you're determining how to present your site and pages, it's best to put the most important information in the part of the Web page the visitor sees first.

In the newspaper business this section of a page is called *above the fold*. In a Web page, it's the first 315 pixels in height. Pixel is a graphic measurement of space.

YOU'LL THANK YOURSELF LATER

If you really want to create effect with a subhead, make it a different color than the text. Adding color to text is covered in Chapter 6.

BUILD A WEB SITE *The Lazy Way*

What you want to include in this above-the-fold area is the name or title of the site, the site logo or graphic, and the area of the site you want to promote. You also should offer some form of navigation in this area. Remember, you want visitors to know where they are at all times. See Figure 5.9 for an example of important information in a site included in the first part of the page that a visitor sees.

Figure 5.9 *The Soccer World Cup site.*

However, you also want to keep this area clutter free. That means you don't want to use too many graphics. If you have text you want your visitors to read, a good rule of thumb is to have no more than half the space taken up with graphics. Also, be sure some text is visible so they can start reading as soon as your site starts loading.

Speaking of graphics, they should be your next consideration. You want your pages to load fast so you should be aware that most Web servers call up four GIFs, a graphic file format, at a time. Therefore, you want to limit these graphics to four or fewer per page.

Along with the text and graphics you use to create your pages, you also need to use white space. A little bit of white space goes a long way in avoiding the appearance of too much stuffed in the area above the fold. Good use of white space keeps your pages from looking cluttered. If your pages look too busy a visitor could get confused and leave. As a starter, try leaving a little bit of white space between the main graphic on your page and the text. You can also place an extra space between paragraphs by placing an extra paragraph tag <P> between them.

Now let's look at some elements to avoid when designing your pages. These are elements that can slow down the loading of your pages or can potentially scare your visitors off.

Nested tables, tables within tables, may look impressive, but they slow the performance of your site considerably. Another type of table to avoid is long vertical columns of tables, for the same reason.

Instead of using either of these methods, try stacking tables on top of each other. When you use this stacked method, you page appears to load faster because the top table loads first, giving your visitors something to read while they wait for the rest of the page to load. CNET's SEARCH.COM site is an excellent example of using stacked tables. It prides itself on being one of the fastest-loading sites of its kind on the Web. See Figure 5.10 for an example of this stacked tables method.

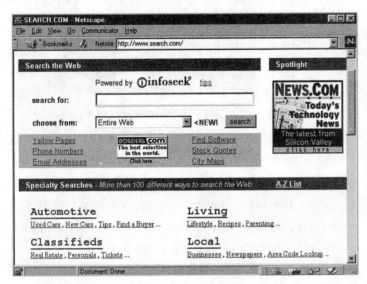

Figure 5.10 *SEARCH.COM site with stacked tables.*

Gimmicks like scrolling text in the status bar can be fun to add to your pages. However, you should avoid them unless you have a good reason for using them. This scrolling text only slows access to your site. If you can't fit the words in this scroll in your text, then you probably don't need them.

For your front door page or home page, avoid using optional plug-ins or browser-specific technologies. This includes audio, video, or animations.

You run the risk of scaring your visitors off when you try to introduce these elements in your home page. They often require a lot of explanation so the visitor can use

QUICK PAINLESS

If you want to draw your visitor's interest to a particular area, you don't have to use graphics. You can vary the size of the type to bring their focus to a specific area.

them. They also require the visitor to have or acquire an extra utility in order to enjoy this extra technology.

Some browsers support all the latest technology and scripts, but some don't. Some visitors will happily install an extra utility to experience what you have to offer, while others will just leave. They can't be bothered to install one more extra program or they just don't have the extra space they want to devote to something they may only use on your site. Therefore, you risk alienating a portion of your visitors. Be aware that it can often take a long time for some plug-ins to download. Some can take as long as 30 minutes.

While the latest technology is cool and can make your pages do cool and exciting things, it's wise to use them with care or to avoid them altogether.

FURNISHINGS MAKE THE SPACE

Prioritize what you want to present and present it in a fashion that lets the visitors know what's most important. One way to do this is with *scaling*. Make what's the most important the biggest, then scale other areas down. When you determine what your priorities are, it's easier to figure out where all the pieces go.

There are several ways you can lay out the elements in your pages to make them more appealing and balanced. One is to lay text out asymmetrically. For instance, you could have two columns of text and other elements in a 30:70 ratio that balances white space and text.

Another method you can use is to stagger sections of text and/or graphics. This stagger method pulls the reader's

QUICK ⬥ PAINLESS

Balancing text and graphics is what makes your site pleasing and keeps your visitors interested. It's easy to get carried away with type and overwhelm your visitors. Alignment, grouping, and asymmetrical presentations of type in harmony with images are the key to achieving this balance.

eyes through chunks of your information. See Figure 5.11 for an example of the use of this staggered approach. The Business Committee for the Arts site groups typographic sections together to make the overall page more appealing.

Figure 5.11   *Business Committee for the Arts site.*

Along with these two approaches to manipulating text to make your site more exciting and easier to read, you can also use typographical emphasis to spice up your content. Bold, italic, underline, and other HTML tags can add emphasis to words or phrases to make them stand out on the page. Used properly, they can enhance your text and help your visitor find important information.

QUICK PAINLESS

When trying to remember when to use italic, bold or larger text size for words, use the following hints:

- Italic—Words you'd emphasize in speech.

- Bold—Words you want as anchors or to assist the reader in finding specific spots.

- Large Text—For words you want to stand out from other text.

IF YOU'RE SO
INCLINED

You can find various scripts to add special elements to your pages at the following sites:

Matt's Script Archive— http://www.worldwidemart.com/scripts

Hot Style 'n The JavaScript Resource— http://www.serve.com/hotstyle

These sites offer pre-made scripts that you can simply insert into your site.

DECORATIONS JAZZ UP A ROOM

Scripting is another way to add elements to your pages or cause things to happen within them. Scripts are mini-programs that function within programs or pages.

There are several different types of scripts used in Web sites, such as Java, ActiveX, CGI, and Perl, to name a few. Each of these scripts adds enhancements to pages or cause activities to happen on a page. For instance, scripts can make images randomly display, add a clock to your page, perform a simple search, add a quiz, create a message board system or forum, or verify credit card information.

Scripting requires a knowledge or understanding of programming. It's much too complicated for the scope of this book; therefore, it won't be covered in detail.

Building a site that looks good involves incorporating many elements and arranging those elements in a pleasing, logical, and accessible manner. The material in this chapter is designed to help you consider all the elements that make up a site that not only entertains your visitors but also encourages them to explore it.

Now that you have some basics under your belt and a better understanding of how to plan and design a successful site, it's time to start learning how to use some of these elements in building your site. Backgrounds play a subtle but vital role in your site, so we'll tackle it next.

six

Backfield in Motion

Backgrounds and fonts are the subtle elements of your site that set the overall mood. They may not seem important, but improper use of either of them can drive visitors away in droves.

Color, both for the background and text, can enhance pages or detract from them. For instance, red text on a black background can be quite hard on the eyes. It also doesn't print well unless the visitor adjusts her browser setting to accommodate and alter what you created. This just defeats what you're trying to do.

On the other hand, using light backgrounds for pages with lots of text makes it easier to read and more appealing to the eyes. See Figure 6.1 for an example of dark text on a light background. The Homework Help site shows how text and background can work together to create a pleasing site.

The key to successful use of background is to keep the contrast in mind. Pages with high contrast between text and background are easier to read.

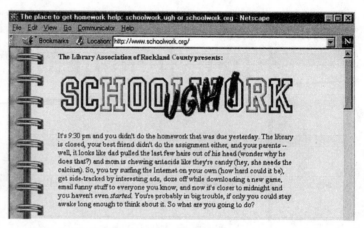

Figure 6.1 *The Homework Help site.*

COLOR BY NUMBER

Understanding how color and backgrounds work in Web pages is essential in building your site. Knowing when and how to use colors for your text and backgrounds will help you create a site visitors will enjoy.

Back in grade school or high school, you learned the primary colors—red, blue, and yellow. To create other colors, you simply combine portions of these primary colors together.

In the real world that is how you create varying colors. In the world of computers and the Web, you use red, green, and blue (RGB) to mix new or other colors.

Colors used in computer graphics are represented by the 0-9 and A-F numbers and letters. These are known as hex codes. Combinations of these digits create shades of colors. The color representation is done three times; once for red, once for green, and once for blue, in that order. When you put together these three in two-digit combinations, you get a six-digit hex code. The computer reads these codes, meshes them together, and creates a single shade of color.

For instance, 0000FF is blue, while 000000 is black. When you change any one of the red, green, or blue levels in these hex codes, you change the color.

With Web pages, some colors are what is called *Web safe*. This means they're read correctly no matter what browser is being used. Hex color codes that begin with 00, 33, 66, 99, CC, or FF are Web-safe colors.

There are 216 colors represented by these hex codes that appear as the color you ask for no matter what type computer or browser you use. These are called non-dithering colors and produce smooth color in graphics and Web pages. These are the same colors Windows and Macintosh operating systems use for their color palettes.

COLOR YOUR WORLD

There are several ways you can create intriguing backgrounds for your pages. The simplest method is to create a background color. Another technique is to use a wallpaper effect to spice up your pages.

IF YOU'RE SO INCLINED

You can find charts containing the various hex codes for colors and Web-safe colors at the following sites:

Hex and Word Color Codes—
www.htmlgoodies.com/
colors.html

Non-Dithering Colors—
www.htmlgoodies.com/
non_dithering_colors.html

Since adding color is the easiest, let's start with it and learn how to add it to your pages. Then we'll learn how to add wallpaper.

You begin by placing the code command immediately following the TITLE command. The code tag is an unpaired tag that is typed like so: <BODY BGCOLOR="#######">. All but one of the number symbols are replaced with the hex code for the color you want for your background. So, if you want a blue background, the code tag would read like this: <BODY BGCOLOR="#0000FF">. The quotation marks are important because they let the Web server know this is a code within a code or to look for a specific file.

That was pretty easy, wasn't it? Now, let's try our hand at adding wallpaper as a background to a page. This will make an image cover your background (for tiled images, see the discussion later).

The first step is to have a background you want to use. You can use one from the programs on your computer or you can grab one from sites on the Web. There are several sites that offer lots of backgrounds to choose from. These wallpaper backgrounds are actually graphic files, either GIFs or JPEGs. If you're real adventurous, you can create your own wallpaper for your backgrounds.

Next, you need to type the code tag after the TITLE command. The command for the background wallpaper is slightly different from the background color command. It's typed like this: <BODY BACKGROUND="image.gif">. You insert the name of the image file in place of image.gif.

The background command overrides the background color command. This happens because wallpaper goes over color. However, the image for the wallpaper often takes a little bit of time to load. Normally, a black screen appears while this image is loading.

You can change this by adding the background color command to the background command. This causes a nice color to display until your wallpaper image wipes it out. Here's how you'd write this command: <BODY BGCOLOR="######" BACKGROUND="image.gif">.

That's all there is to it. It's not as hard as you thought.

LET YOUR WEB EDITOR DO IT FOR YOU

Some HTML editors offer wallpaper options and some don't. Most, however, do offer a tool or options to add background color. If they don't, you can simply add the command tag and hex color code described in the previous section.

For the editors that offer wizards to assist you in setting up your pages, such as HotDog Express, you simply choose the wallpaper you want to use from the options it gives you. Most of these type editors also give you an option to add your own wallpaper choices. See Figure 6.2 for an example of the choices that HotDog Express gives you for background wallpapers.

In the other editors, you'll have to insert the code for the wallpaper and possibly also for the background color if you choose to use one. A few offer a template to select a background color, but none of these text editors offer an option to insert a background wallpaper.

YOU'LL THANK YOURSELF LATER

Placing image-based or pattern backgrounds behind text often makes the text hard to read. You can fix this easily by either using a different graphic or by blurring the background. You'll need an image program so you can use its editing tools to alter the background image you want to use.

Figure 6.2 *HotDog Express wallpaper options.*

TILED IMAGES

Some designers use *tiled images* for backgrounds. Basically, tiled images are textured images that are repeated over each other several times.

These tiled images can create some interesting background effects on your pages. However, unless your heart is absolutely set on using them, it is better to use a wallpaper background or a background color.

The process for creating these type images is tricky and requires an additional image program such as Photoshop Pro. You have to make sure the image flows smoothly when tiled and that there are no seams in it.

Tiled images make pages load much slower than other images. It is always wise to have others check your results before you post them to the Web. A more in-depth discussion of tiling images is covered in Chapter 9.

FRIENDLY FONTS

Everything you create in Web pages requires some kind of command tag. This is also true for fonts.

The Font Size command is a paired tag. Using this command you can control your text size. HTML gives you 12 font sizes to use with the Font Size command. These are +6 through +1 and -1 through -6. The +6 is the largest

IF YOU'RE SO
INCLINED

You can find pre-made tiled images at the following sites:

A tiled image archive—
http://www.plig.org/xwinmon/tiles

Another tiled image archive—
http://www.me.mtu.edu/cael/backgrounds/index.html

while -6 is the smallest. The command is typed like so: <FONT SIZE="*size*">Your text here</FONT>. Notice the ending tag only requires </FONT>. You can add SIZE, but it's not necessary for this command. If you want a relatively large font, the command might look like this: <FONT SIZE="+3"> Your text here</FONT>.

In addition to controlling the size of your text, you can control how it appears on the page. There are individual commands for the various ways you can align text on a page. The following are the alignment commands you'll use:

- Center—<CENTER>Your text here</CENTER>
- Align Right—<P ALIGN="right">Your text here</P>

Left-aligned text is the default alignment because most text is normally written and read that way.

Notice the paragraph tag is used to align text to the right. This is because it's generally paragraphs of text that get aligned to the right. Whenever you add a subcommand to an unpaired tag, you have to close the command. In this instance, P is the main command, while ALIGN=right is the subcommand.

Along with changing the font sizes and aligning text, you can also add color to your text. This involves a command to change the text color combined with a hex color code. With this command you can add color to a full page of text or just to specific words.

To color a whole page of text, the command is: <TEXT="#######">. Therefore, if you want the text to be the color blue, the command would look like this:

When you're presenting long columns of type, such as information about products, you can break up the columns visually by varying the paragraph colors.

<TEXT="#0000FF">. This command immediately follows the Title command.

If you want to change the color of just one word or just a few words, the command is: <FONT COLOR= "######">the word or words here</FONT>. You can use this command with all the Header and other text size commands.

Be aware that some visitors adjust their browsers to read sites with fonts they select. When they change their preferences in their browsers, it can override the settings you make when designing your site. The upside is that some new HTML versions can handle style sheets that allow you to use a wider range of fonts. These include the fonts of Palatino, Times, and others. These different fonts and their use won't be covered in this book. If you like you can try using different fonts and test the results when you view your pages before hanging them.

LET YOUR WEB EDITOR DO IT FOR YOU

Most of the HTML editors offer you an option to change the font color and to change font sizes. Generally, they offer you a command in the menu bar or an icon to select. The ones that offer wizards give you the option to select your text colors when you initially set up your pages with them. Most of them let you choose your font styles and sizes or alter them using an icon.

For the WYSIWYG editors such as HotDog Express, you can select your text colors but you can't select font styles or sizes. The text editors like 1-4-All let you choose all of these and customize them to your preferences.

With this particular editor, you can adjust the font size or the font color by highlighting the text to select it and then by selecting Fonts from the Tag Dialog menu item. The program gives you a dialog box that lets you select the font size and color you want for your highlighted text. When you make your selections and click on the OK button, the tags are added around the highlighted text.

Most of the Web editors offer you easy text manipulation. They generally give you menus and dialog boxes to assist you in this area. Refer to the help files for the program you're using to learn how it handles this element of designing pages.

PROJECT

Let's create a page with a title, background color, background wallpaper, header, and a few lines of text. We'll use all of the commands we've learned so far.

The lazy way—or smart way, depending on how you look at it—to make text and background manipulations is to let the Web editor do all or as much of the work as possible. However, rather than use an editor that does everything in the wizard for us and where we have less control, let's use a text editor with most of the tags in icons for easy use. I'm going to use the 1-4-All program for this project.

Each editor has it's own way of helping you create pages. If it's an editor that guides you through templates, follow the steps it takes you through. If it's more

of a text editor, you'll need to insert text between tags provided or use the icons to insert tags and type your text between the tags.

Don't get nervous. Just follow these easy steps:

1. Open the editor you want to use.

2. First, create a title for the page. Let's call our page **The PaintGuy**.

   For this example, we're going to start building a page for a hypothetical business. Therefore, we're going to type in the name of the business between the title tag.

3. Next, let's set up our background color. First, we need to pick a color to use. Let's use antique white with the hex code of FAEBD7. (Remember, there was a sidebar that told you where you could find these hex color codes on the Web.)

   If your editor lets you choose a color in a template or dialog box, select the color you want from your background.

4. Now we need to type this code in if we're using a text Web page editor or select the color we want if we're using a WYSIWYG editor. 1-4-All doesn't have an icon or the option to choose a background color, so I have to type the command tag in. Type <BODY BGCOLOR="#FAEBD7">.

5. Next, we want to also add a wallpaper. So, first we need to have a graphics file we can use as our wallpaper.

I chose one of the wallpaper files I found in the Windows files. (I had to convert it to a .gif format to use it because it was in a .bmp format. I did this by using an image program called Photoshop Pro. I simply opened the file in that program and then selected Save As from the File menu and saved it as a .gif format with the same file name. Graphics formats are covered in more detail in Chapter 9.)

6. Type the tag for the background wallpaper BACK-GROUND= after the <BODY BGCOLOR="#FAEBD7". In place of the last angle bracket, insert a space. Then use the insert image icon to place the image address in the code or type the path and file name for the image. Therefore the whole command for the background color and wall paper will look like this: <BODY BGCOLOR="#FAEBD7" BACKGROUND= "C:/directory name/program name/file name>. In my case it looks like this: <BODY BGCOLOR="#FAEBD7" BACKGROUND="C:/Program Files/htmlnotes/Blue Rivets.gif">.

7. Now that we have our background established, let's add a header. We don't want our header to be too big so we're going to select Header Two, H2. Click on the H2 and insert the text for your header between the tags. We also want our header centered so we're also going to select the Center alignment icon.

8. Then we type the text we want as our header in between these H2 and CENTER tags. This is our hypothetical business page so the first header is going to be **The PaintGuy.**

9. Next, we also want this header in a different color than the rest of the text so we need to insert the commands to make it so. Highlight the text and select Tag Dialogs and Fonts from the menu bar if you're using 1-4-All. If you're using a different editor, select the icon or command that changes the font color. Then choose a color from the color palette the program gives you. In this case I chose red.

10. Next, we need to add a few lines of text to our page. First click on the paragraph icon to tell the program you're starting a paragraph. Then type some text.

11. We have our title, background, header, and a color change on the color. We also now have some text to work with. Highlight the text to select it and then select the editing tool to give it a font size. In 1-4-All this is the Tags Dialog/Fonts in the menu bar. Designate the size you want for the fonts and a color if you also want to change the color. I chose to change the first two words in my paragraph to red and a +3 size, while choosing a +2 size and the color blue for the rest of my text.

You've begun creating a page using an HTML editor. Go take a look at it. There is an option that lets you pre-

Before you start this project, put in your favorite CD. Then when you've finished the steps here, treat yourself to a gift. Go to the local music store and get yourself a new CD by your favorite artist. You deserve a pat on the back and a reward!

The Lazy Way

view your page. It's usually an icon or a menu bar item. See Figure 6.3 for an example of how the code looks in the editor and Figure 6.4 for how the page actually looks. Figure 6.4 shows how the page looks using the preview feature in the 1-4-All editor.

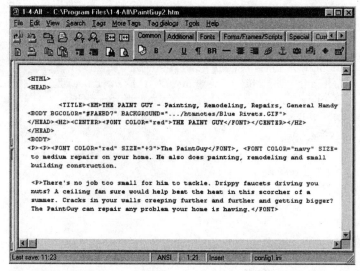

Figure 6.3 *The code for the project in the 1-4-All HTML editor edit screen.*

You're now well on your way to building a Web site. You've taken the first steps by creating this beginning page and adding a title, header, backgrounds, and text. You're starting to see that it's not so hard building a Web site after all.

But you've just begun. It's time to move on and learn a few other elements you can use in your site. The next step is to learn how to add tables to your pages.

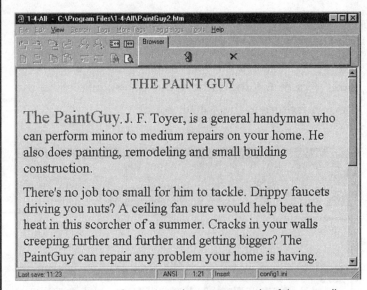

Figure 6.4 *The page in the preview mode of the 1-4-All HTML editor.*

Part 3

Footloose and Clutter Free

seven

Making a List, Checking It Twice

One element that is common in many Web pages is lists. There are many reasons to use them in your site. One reason is they break up large areas of text and make a better presentation.

You use lists for a table of contents, definitions, cross-references, menu items, or to bullet a series of similar items. If you want to include your résumé in your site, you'll likely have a list of your accomplishments or attributes. You can even use lists to link to other areas or pages in your site. Lists also come in handy when you have several related links you want to include in your site.

LISTS FOR ALL OCCASIONS

With HTML documents or pages, there are three kinds of lists you can use—definition lists, ordered lists, and unordered lists. *Definition lists* are just as they sound—lists that contain a term with a definition following it. *Ordered lists* are either numbered lists or lists of items that occur in a specific order or ranking of importance. For instance, step-by-step instructions are an ordered list. An *unordered list* is a random list of items usually displayed with bullets.

In addition to creating these lists, you can attach format attributes to them. For instance, you can make the lists Bold, Italic, or Underlined. You can also set these lists up in a table. See Chapter 8 for instructions on creating a table.

In HTML pages there are special tags for each of these different types of lists. Following are those tags and how they work.

DEFINITION LISTS

Definition lists are like glossaries. The following are tags for this type list:

- <DL> </DL>—Tells the program that you are starting and ending a definition list.

- <DT> Definition Term—Indicates that the following item is a definition term. Needs no closing tag.

- <DD>—Indicates that everything following it is a definition description. Needs no closing tag.

The code for a sample definition list in it might look something like this:

```
<DL> HTML Terms
<DT> Tags <DD> come in paired and unpaired and are
formatting codes.
<DT> Hyperlinks <DD> are links to other areas in
your pages or to other pages on the Web. </DL>
```

See Figure 7.1 for an example of how this code looks in a Web page.

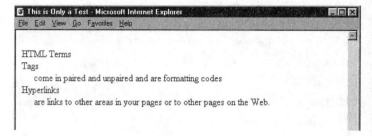

Figure 7.1 *Preview in a browser of a definition list.*

ORDERED LISTS

Ordered lists are numbered lists. You use these for items that must appear in a specific order. You'd use these lists for step-by-step instructions or recipes. The following are the tags you use to create this type of list:

- <OL> </OL>—Begins and ends the list in HTML documents.

- <LI> List Item—The items in your ordered list ranked by importance or number. Needs no closing tag.

An ordered list might look something like this if you were to do the coding yourself. The numbers are automatically embedded into the document. You don't need to insert them yourself.

```
<OL> Ordered Lists
<LI> Begin with the opening tag for ordered lists
and then type in your list name.
<LI> Add the tag for the list item and follow it
with the list item.
<LI> Continue on with the list item tags and list
items until you complete your list.
<LI> End your list with the end list tag. </OL>
```

See Figure 7.2 for an example of how this code looks in a Web page.

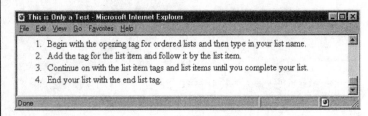

Figure 7.2 *Preview in a browser of this Ordered list.*

UNORDERED LISTS

Unordered lists are bulleted lists. These lists include items that don't have to appear in a specific order.

Following are the code tags for this type list:

- <UL> </UL>—This one works the same way as the ordered list as far as placement of tags goes.

- <LI> List item—Used with the <UL> </UL> tags. This bullets your list items. It needs no closing tag.

Entering the tags for an unordered list works the same way as for the ordered list, substituting UL for OL within the command angle brackets. The bullets are automatically inserted in the document you're creating. However, they won't appear as part of the source code, but will show up in the viewed document. See Figure 7.3 for an example of how this code looks in a page.

Following is how you might use this list:

<UL>Unordered List

<LI>Insert a list item

<LI>Insert another list item

<LI>Be sure to close the list</UL>

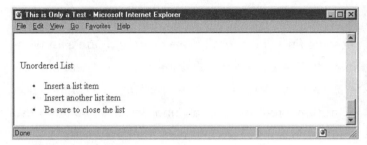

Figure 7.3 *Preview in a browser of this bulleted list in a page.*

MENU LISTS AND DIRECTORY LISTS

A *menu list* is a list of items, usually choices limited to one item per line. There aren't a lot of pages that use this type of list, but it's included here in case you ever find a need for it.

To create a menu list, you perform the same steps as for unordered lists. The beginning tag for this list is <MENU>.

Directory lists are generally used for displaying a list of filenames. Like the menu list, this list uses the same steps as the unordered lists. The code for this type list is a paired tag. You'll need to begin and end this list with these tags: <DIR></DIR>.

The Directory list and the Menu list display identical in pages. Unless you look at the source code, you'll probably never know the difference. These two lists appear in pages as unordered lists. They appear as bulleted lists.

QUICK ⬛ PAINLESS

Since the Directory and Menu lists look identical to an unordered, bulleted list when viewed in pages, the easiest way to create these lists is to just use the unordered list codes and format.

LISTS WITHIN LISTS

At some time you might have a need to create a list within a list. These are also called *nested lists*. There are several ways you can create these lists. One is a combination of a numbered list with an unordered or bulleted list. Another way is to combine two unordered lists.

Here's how the code looks for numbered lists with a bulleted nested list:

```
<OL>
<LI>Category item
<UL><LI>Subcategory item
<LI>Another subcategory item
</OL></UL>
```

LET YOUR WEB EDITOR DO IT FOR YOU

Creating lists is simple when you use an HTML editor. To create a numbered list, click the Numbered List icon in the toolbar. This icon looks like a page with a numbered list on it. The editor gives you a dialog box that asks you to fill in the number of items in your list, the type of bullet you want to use.

Not all the editors use the same icons. Review the toolbar for the editor you choose and familiarize yourself with its icons. If you place your cursor over each icon, a tooltip pops up to tell you what that icon is and does.

In addition, some editors give you a dialog box and walk you through the steps to create a list while others simply insert the code. Then you must supply the text and add the code where needed.

After you've indicated how you want the list to appear, click on the OK button. The tags are added to your page and you can then enter the list information.

Creating a definition list is just as easy. First, choose the point where you want the list to go. Next, click on the DL icon in the toolbar and type in the title for your definition list between the tags. Then click on the DT icon in the toolbar and type your Definition Term, followed by clicking on the DD icon and typing in the definition. Continue clicking on the DT icon, typing the definition term, clicking on DD, and typing the definition for each term you want in your list. To end the list, press enter twice.

To create the ordered/unordered combination of a list within a list, follow these steps:

1. Type your whole list.

2. Highlight all the main headings of your list and click on the Ordered List icon to apply it to these headings.

3. Next, for all the subordinate items in your list—the items that go in the list within the list—highlight them and click on the Unordered List icon to apply it.

If you prefer to create an unordered/unordered list combination, follow these steps:

1. Type your whole list.

2. Highlight the whole list to select it and click on the Undordered list icon to apply the bullet style tags.

3. Next, select the subordinate groups and click on the

Increase Indent icon from the toolbar. In the 1-4-All editor, this icon shows lines on a page with some of the lines indented. Other editors might use an icon that looks like a page with lines on it and an arrow pointing in to indicate indented lines.

If you want to add other formatting to these lists, simply highlight the words in the list that you want to format and choose the format you want to apply. For instance, you can add bold by selecting the text you want to bold and clicking on the Bold icon or inserting the codes by hand. If you want to make a list item a link, highlight it and click on the Link icon. Fill in the text boxes in the dialog box and your list item is now a link.

PROJECT

Creating lists in your pages is one of the easiest techniques to perform. Let's practice for our site. Open your editor and follow along with me as we create a list. I'll be using the 1-4-All HTML editor for this project.

1. Click on the Definition List (DL) icon in the toolbar.

2. Next to the <DL> tag type Favorite Pets. This is going to be the title for our list.

3. Then press the Enter key to get to the next line. Don't worry about that </DL> tag. We're going to keep pushing that tag to the end.

4. Now click on the Definition Term (DT) icon, and type the first term—Dog. Press the Enter key again to get to the next line.

QUICK ☜☞ PAINLESS

To reformat existing text as a bulleted list or numbered list, select the paragraphs you want to format and then click on the Bulleted List or the Numbered List icon in the tool bar.

5. Click on the Definition Description (DD) icon and type the following: "a furry animal that comes in various sizes and breeds and that is loyal and barks to warn its owner of intruders". Press the Enter key to get to the next line.

6. Follow steps 3 and 4 for the following terms and definitions:

   ■ Cats—A small furry animal that is independent and purrs when content.

   ■ Bird—A small animal that can fly and sings when contented.

   ■ Fish—Small icthyoid that lives in a glass aquarium and provides certain proteins to hungry cats.

   Press the Enter key to get to the next line.

7. Your list is finished now. Click on the Preview icon and see how it will appear in your page. See Figure 7.4 for an example of how this code appears in your page.

   If you want to spice your list up with format attributes or make your list items link to other pages within your site or on the Web, let's continue with our steps and learn how.

8. To add some format attributes to your list, first highlight the words you want to format.

9. Let's make the list title and all the definition terms bold. Click on the Bold icon. Because we've already typed the list out, you'll have to bold each item separately.

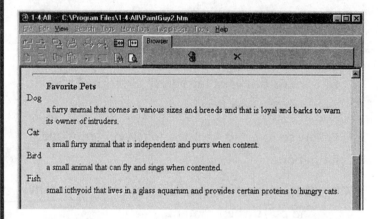

Figure 7.4 *Preview of list code for a project in a browser.*

10. To make your list items a link, again, highlight the item you want to make a link. Let's make the definition terms the linking words.

11. After you highlight one of the definition terms, click on the Link icon.

12. In the dialog box, type in the address for the link.

For the purpose of this project we're going to use imaginary addresses. In your real documents you would use the address to another page or to another site on the Web. This address would be one that's related to the information in your list.

The addresses we'll use here will be the http://www.dog.com, http://www.cats.com, http://www.birds.com, and http://www.fish.com, respectively.

13. If your definition term is not in the Text or Description box, type it in. Otherwise, click on the OK button.

Your attributes and links are now inserted around your definition terms. Let's go look at how they'll appear on the page.

14. Click on the Preview button. See Figure 7.5 for an example of how this code should look as you're creating the list from these steps and Figure 7.6 is an example of how the list looks on the page when you preview it using the editor's preview function.

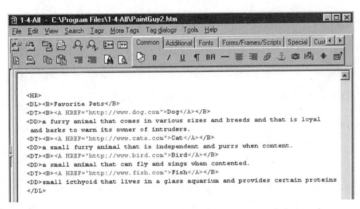

Figure 7.5 The 1-4-All HTML editor page with list codes and list entered.

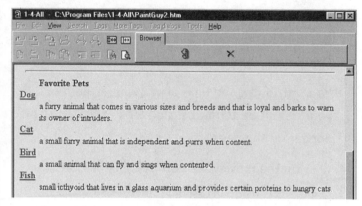

Figure 7.6 *Preview view of the list created in the 1-4-All editor.*

EXTRA CREDIT PROJECT

You have a little practice under your belt with creating lists. Now let's use what we've learned to create a recipe in a list. Here's a short recipe we're going to use:

Chocolate Silk Pie

Ingredients:

1 box silken tofu, soft

1 bag milk chocolate chips (not semisweet chips)

1 graham cracker crust

To bake:

1. Blend tofu in blender or food processor until smooth.

2. Melt chocolate chips in microwave.

3. Pour melted chocolate into blended tofu.

4. Mix until smooth and uniform.

5. Pour into graham cracker crust.

6. Chill for at least 2 hours.

If you're feeling particularly confident, see if you can create this list yourself. A hint: The first part is an unordered list while the second part is an ordered list.

For those of us that would like a little more practice, follow these instructions:

1. Type the name of the list: Chocolate Silk Pie.

2. Type the first Category: Ingredients:.

3. Click on the Unordered list icon to start the list.

4. Space down to the next line and click on the List Item icon.

5. Type the first item in the recipe list after the <LI> tag: 1 box silken tofu, soft.

6. Repeat steps 4 and 5 for each of the ingredients.

   (Each time you space down, you push the closing unordered list tag down. Be sure it ends up at the end of this ingredients list.)

7. Type the category name for the instructions: To back:.

8. Click on the Ordered List icon to begin the ordered list.

9. Space down and click on the List Item icon.

10. Type the first instruction (don't forget you don't need to type the numbers. The program will do it for you).

11. Repeat steps 9 and 10 for all the instructions.

12. Make sure the closing ordered list tag ends up at the end of your instruction list.

13. Now go look at what you created. Click on the preview option in your editor. See Figure 7.7 for an example of how this recipe should look in a Web page.

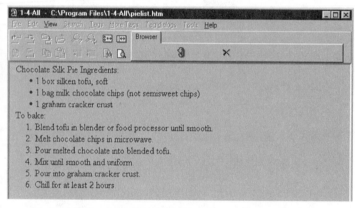

Figure 7.7 *Preview of the Chocolate Silk Pie recipe in the 1-4-All HTML editor.*

That's it. You're done!

I told you that was going to be easy. Take what you've learned in this chapter and create lists to organize information and design interesting pages for your site. Using an HTML editor you can create numbered, ordered, unordered, and nested lists. You can also use these lists for links to other pages or create links from the items in your lists. You're the list expert now!

Oh master of lists, you are beyond compare. You deserve a treat. As your reward, you should make this amazingly simple pie and indulge yourself.

The Lazy Way

Now that you have tables and lists under your belt, it's time to start learning some more advanced-type techniques for building your site. The next section will teach you how to use images in your site to jazz it up and make it more appealing to your visitors.

Turning the Tables

In your job you've probably seen, worked with, or had to set up a table of information. Tables are a great way to organize information and present it in a pleasing manner.

With Web pages you can use tables in them in much the same way you've seen them used at your place of work. But, there are many other ways you can use them too.

On your Web site you can use them as a presentation technique. For instance, you can use tables to create a horizontal list of links. A horizontal list is links side by side instead of one on each line. You can also use a horizontal list as a way to present groups of information on your pages. You can use tables for calendars, posting resumes, or offsetting graphics. The list of possibilities is endless.

All you need to do now is learn how to use the commands to create your own tables. Then you can apply what you learn to the ideas you have and create some exciting pages. See Figure 8.1 for an example of a table used in a Web site. This designer used many of the elements that will be covered in this chapter to create this table. She used background colors, links, and column spanning to creating an exciting table.

IF YOU'RE SO
INCLINED

If you'd like to learn the various possibilities of how you can use tables to present information in your site, take a look at the source code on several of your favorites sites or any of the sites you visit over the course of a week or two. (You can view this source code by selecting View, Page Source in Netscape or View, Source from Internet Explorer.) This gives you hints on how others are using tables.

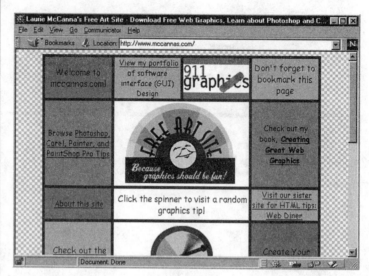

Figure 8.1 *Laurie McCanna's Free Art site with a table as part of the site.*

SETTING THE TABLE

When you're ready to place tables in your Web pages, you need to know the commands and the steps to take to create them. The main command is the paired tags <TABLE></TABLE>.

Typing this command around your table information gives you the beginning and ending tags only. You need to finish telling the program what else you want it to do. So, you need a few more tags.

You also need a <CAPTION></CAPTION> paired tag. And, you need the <TD></TD> and <TR></TR> paired tags.

Let's take a look at what each of these tags does:

■ <TABLE></TABLE>—Begins and ends the entire table.

- <CAPTION></CAPTION>—Places a caption on your table.

- <TD></TD>—Stands for Table Data. This tag is placed before each item in your table. However, you only need </TD> before the ending TABLE tag.

- <TR></TR>—Stands for Table Row. You use this tag when you want a new row. Again, only one </TR> is needed at the end of the table information.

Using just these commands gives you a pretty simple, plain Jane table. Now if you want to spice up your table, you're going to need to take a few extra steps.

There are many different ways you can create fancier tables. For instance, you can add borders, space the cells, align the text within the cells and rows, add padding to the cells, cause cells to be activated as links, place images in cells, frame images, or put a table within a table. Each one of these added elements calls for a separate command.

We'll learn what each of these codes is, then later we'll learn how to create a couple of tables in our pages. Let the show begin.

Following are the main codes you use to create tables:

- Border—<TABLE BORDER="number of pixels">

- Spacing—CELLSPACING="number of pixels"

- Padding—CELLPADDING="number of pixels">

- Alignment—<TD ALIGN="alignment"> your info

The CELLSPACING and CELLPADDING tags are included as part of the TABLE BORDER command; therefore,

QUICK ☻ PAINLESS

As you are creating these tables for your pages, remember—a table is a series of columns and rows which the server and programs refer to as cells.

YOU'LL THANK YOURSELF LATER

Before trying to create a table in your pages, you can save yourself a lot of time and frustration if you draw it on paper first. This helps you see where the rows need to break and helps you get the codes in the right places.

they don't require opening and closing angle brackets. Just be sure to place the closing bracket after the end of the CELLPADDING figure.

<BORDER> lets the Web server know how big the border should be. If you don't want the line, use the number 0. <CELLSPACING> tells the server how much space to place in the cells, while <CELLPADDING> indicates how much padding you need in each cell. Padding is the amount of space between the contents of a cell and the border of a cell. And, of course, you know what <ALIGN> and <CENTER> do from previous commands.

So if you want to create a table listing various breeds of cats and you want that table to have borders and have the breeds centered in the cells, here is how the code would look:

```
<TABLE BORDER="3" CELLSPACING="1" CELLPADDING="1">
<CAPTION>Cat Breeds</CAPTION>
<TD ALIGN="center" Siamese
<TD ALIGN="center" Mancoon
<TD ALIGN="center" Burmese<TR>
<TD ALIGN="center" Bengal
<TD ALIGN="center" Persian
<TD ALIGN="center" Occicat<TR>
</TR>
</TD>
</TABLE>
```

See Figure 8.2 for an example of this simple table.

YOU'LL THANK YOURSELF LATER

Don't forget to close all your paired tags. If you run into a problem with your tables, check for this first. It's a common mistake.

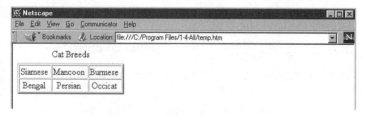

Figure 8.2 *View of Cat Breeds table in a browser.*

When you want to activate a cell in your tables as a link, the command you use is: <TD ALIGN="alignment"><A HREF="link address">Name for link</A>. So, if you wanted to link any of the above cat breeds to a page of information about that breed, you'd use that code instead. It might look like this: <TD ALIGN="center"><A HREF="http://www.siamese.com/">Siamese Cats</A>. If your keyword for the link changes and becomes longer, you'll need to adjust the CELLSPACING and CELLPADDING to accommodate the longer text. See Figure 8.3 for an example of creating links within table cells.

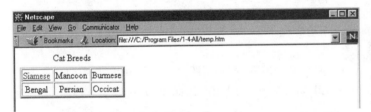

Figure 8.3 *View of Cat Breeds table with a link made of one of the elements in the table.*

If you want to place images in your table instead of text, that's fairly easy to accomplish too. You follow a <TD> command with an image command. For instance, <TD ALIGN="center"><IMG SRC="image.gif">.

When you just want to place a frame around an image you use the table commands. The commands would look like this:

```
<TABLE BORDER="number of pixels">
<TD ALIGN="center"><IMG SRC="image.gif">
</TD></TABLE>
```

See Figure 8.4 for an example of an image placed in a table.

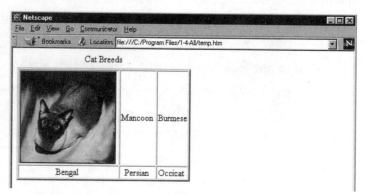

Figure 8.4   *The Cat Breeds table with an image in a table to create a pleasing display.*

Placement of the Table Row <TR> command is crucial. Be sure you place it where you want a new row to start. You can place it in a line of its own or start or end a line with it. If you start a line with it, follow it with the commands for the Table Data <TD>. Just make sure you use this command to indicate when a new row is to start. Be sure to close this tag at the end of your table.

If the image gets shoved into the upper left corner of the cell, you can easily fix it so that it centers the image in the cell. Simply place the <TR> tag in front of the <TD> tag that commands the image. The code would change to this:

```
<TABLE BORDER="20">
<TR><TD ALIGN="center"><IMG SRC="cat.gif"></TR></TD>
</TABLE>
```

You can put just about anything in a table. These commands simply surround the items with a frame.

Earlier you were cautioned against using nested tables in your pages. And you shouldn't. However, just in case you can't resist, here's a short primer on the code to use to place a table within a table.

```
<TABLE BORDER="number of pixels" CELLPADDING="number
of pixels" CELLSPACING="number of pixels">
<TD>
```

```
<TABLE BORDER="number of pixels" CELLPADDING="number
of pixels" CELLSPACING="number of pixels">
<TD>2nd table</TD>
<TD>2nd table</TD>
<TR>
<TD>2nd table</TD>
<TD>2nd table</TD>
</TR>
</TABLE>
```

See Figure 8.5 for an example of a table within a table.

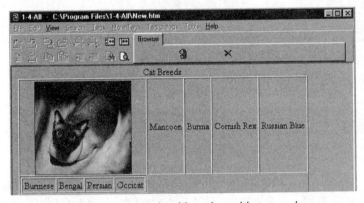

Figure 8.5 *Cat Breeds table with a table inserted.*

When you want to place a table within a table, place a new <TABLE BORDER="number of pixels" CELLSPAC-ING="number of pixels" CELLPADDING="number of pix-els"> command where you want the new table to start. In the cat table pictured in Figure 8.5 the code looks like this:

```
<TABLE BORDER="3" CELLSPACING="1" CELLPADDING="1">
<CAPTION>Cat Breeds</CAPTION>
<TD ALIGN="center"> <A
HREF="http://www.siamese.com"><IMG
SRC="../../MSOffice/Winword/Docs/Build a
Site/siamesecat.jpg" ALT="Siamese cat picture"
ALIGN="MIDDLE" BORDER="2"></A>
<TD ALIGN="center"> Mancoon
<TD ALIGN="center"> Burma
```

continues

continued

```
<TD ALIGN="center"> Cornish Rex
<TD ALIGN="center"> Russian Blue
<TR>
<TD><TABLE BORDER="3" CELLSPACING="1" CELL-
PADDING="1">
<TD ALIGN="center"> Burmese
<TD ALIGN="center"> Bengal
<TD ALIGN="center"> Persian
<TD ALIGN="center"> Occicat
</TR>
</TD>
</TABLE>
```

DRESSING THE TABLE

When you're ready to get really fancy with your tables, there are a few other things you can do to dress them up. The elements covered in this section deal with the spacing of the cells in your table.

The first command we'll learn is Column Span. It lets you span text across several columns or cells of your table. The Column Span command is <TD ALIGN="center" COLSPAN="number of columns">Your text goes here<TR>.

Therefore, if you have a table that has three columns and you want a header or topic to span across those three columns, you can write the code like this:

```
<TABLE BORDER="3" CELLSPACING="3" CELLPADDING="3>

<TD ALIGN="center" COLSPAN="3">Your topic here<TR>

<TD ALIGN="center">Your text
<TD ALIGN="center>Your text
<TD ALIGN="center>Your text
</TD>
</TR>
</TABLE>
```

See Figure 8.6 for an example of the Column Span command. In this example, the column spans three of the four columns in the second table.

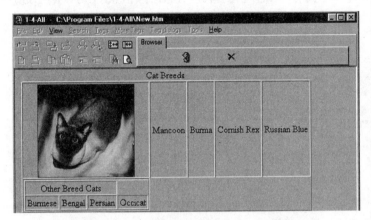

Figure 8.6 *Cat Breeds table with the COLSPAN command used to create a topic for the second table.*

If you had only spanned across two or the three columns, you would need to place another TD cell before the first TR command. Otherwise the span would go too far.

Now let's see how we can span rows instead of columns. The command for this technique is <TD ROWS-PAN="number of-rows" ALIGN="center" WIDTH="number of pixels">Your topic here. With this command you have to tell the server the number of rows to span and the width you want to make this Row Span.

There are two ways that you can designate the Width for this Row Span. One is in number of pixels. If you still don't understand pixels, then you can use a percentage

YOU'LL THANK YOURSELF LATER

A technique to make creating tables with column and row spanning elements easier is to create each table separately. Make sure each table has its own end command. Then cut and paste the table elements to get the final effect.

in relation to the width of the screen. In other words, you can set the width to represent a percentage of the total width of the computer screen. So you could make the width 10% which the server reads to make the Row Span 10% of the total screen. Actually, using this percentage method helps when you're trying to define the space your tables will occupy on your pages. It helps keep the cells more equal between the various browsers and screen settings.

Of course, you can use both the Column Span and Row Span together in the same table. It's a little bit more difficult and will take some preplanning on your part to make sure you get all the commands in the right place. The best advice I can give you is to type the code, test it, and correct any areas that aren't working.

Using the Column Span command, you can create a calendar. It's a simple procedure using the simple table commands with the COLSPAN command. Here's how the code might look:

```
<TABLE BORDER="3" CELLSPACING="3" CELLPADDING="3">
<TD COLSPAN="7" ALIGN="center"><B>JULY 1998</B><TR>

<TD ALIGN="center">Sun
<TD ALIGN="center">Mon
<TD ALIGN="center">Tue
<TD ALIGN="center">Wed
<TD ALIGN="center">Thu
<TD ALIGN="center">Fri
<TD ALIGN="center">Sat
<TR>

<TD ALIGN="center">
<TD ALIGN="center">
<TD ALIGN="center">
<TD ALIGN="center">1
<TD ALIGN="center">2
<TD ALIGN="center">3
```

```
<TD ALIGN="center">4
<TR>
```

(and so on through the rest of the days, ending with the closing tags.)

See, that wasn't so hard. Most of the time, the effects in Web pages look much harder than the techniques themselves are.

One other element you can add to your tables is color. This involves adding the Background Color command and the hex color code for the color you want to use. The command looks like this: <TD BGCOLOR="#######">Your text or graphic. Refer to Chapter 6 for a reminder about color and color codes.

Just as you can add background colors to tables you can also add color to the text within tables. It's a simple matter of adding the FONT COLOR command. The code looks like this: <FONT COLOR="#######">Your text</FONT>. Therefore if you have a table that has background colors and font colors the code might look like this:

```
<TABLE BORDER="3" CELLSPACING="3" CELLPADDING="3">
<TD BGCOLOR="#0000ff"><FONT
COLOR="#80051">Siamese</FONT>
```

Now you're armed with all the codes you need to start creating a variety of tables for your pages. You can use these codes to create exciting effects on your site.

LET YOUR WEB EDITOR DO IT FOR YOU

If you're lazy like me, you hate to spend all that time typing in all those codes. Thank heaven for Web editors—they make the job so much easier.

Most of the editors, even the text editors, give you a tool to help you set up your tables. Generally, this is an icon you click on. When you click on the icon, the program gives you a dialog box to help you fill in the values for the table, such as Number of Rows, Number of Columns, Border Size, Cell Spacing, Cell Padding, and Alignment. Some of them even offer the option of adding color to your table. You can make many of the table adjustments all at once.

Of course, each program has its own way of helping you set up tables. Click on the tool it offers. Then just adjust or enter the information it calls for in the dialog box it gives you.

If the editor doesn't offer an option to insert a certain code you want for your table, you'll have to add the code yourself. For instance, if the editor doesn't offer the option to create links of the cells, you simply add that code in the appropriate place.

Let's take a look at how to create a table in the HTML Helper editor. First, we need to select all the options for our table; set our column and row numbers, font size and screen width; set cell spacing and cell padding, border size, and alignment within the cells; and then choose the colors for the background, font, and borders. When we finish making our selections, we need to click on the Make It button to insert the table in our edit page.

The editor then enters all the codes into the edit page for us and we simply have to insert our text or images in the areas indicated. See Figure 8.7 for an

example of how the code is inserted with prompts to enter the information we want to appear in the page.

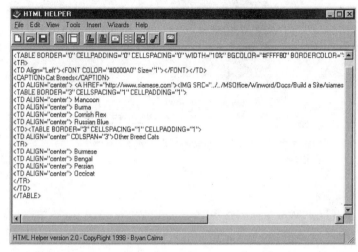

Figure 8.7 *HTML Helper edit page with table commands entered.*

By default, this table will appear justified to the left margin of the page. To center it in our page, we need to add one more command around the table commands. This is the CENTER command. Simply type <CENTER> before the table commands and </CENTER> after, then end tags for the table.

After we enter our text or images in the appropriate places, we need to view the page to make sure everything is working the way we want it. Each editor has its own preview option. Click on that option and the page is opened in your browser. See Figure 8.8 for an example of how the table looks in the preview mode.

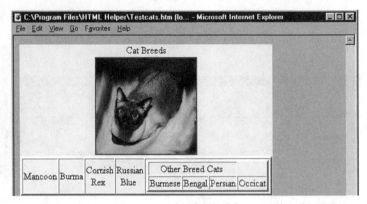

Figure 8.8 *Preview mode of the table created in the HTML Helper editor.*

That was so easy! Before long we'll have our site created and ready to hang.

PROJECT

Tables can be rather intimidating because they look complicated. However, when you use an HTML editor they're much easier to create in your pages. Let's create a couple to get some practice.

First we'll create a simple table, then we'll add some color and links to it. Begin by opening an HTML editor. For this project, I'm going to use the HTML Notes editor. We're going to create a table about dogs. Not every editor handles tables the same way. Be sure to check the help files and documentation for the editor you choose to learn how it works. Also, it might take some trial and error experimenting to get your editor to create the table you want. Just experiment with the tags and preview your results until you get it the way you want.

Follow along with me using these steps:

1. Select the Insert Table icon from the toolbar (or insert a table however your HTML editor requires you to).

2. Enter the values you want for the table. For the Page Width let's use 60%.

3. Next, set the table up for two columns and four rows.

4. Then we need to set the border thickness. We'll set it to 4.

5. Set the Table Alignment to center.

6. Set the Cell Alignment to center.

7. The last item in this dialog box is called Cell <i>Valignment</i>. Cell Valignment adjusts the text within the cell to top, middle, or bottom. We'd like our text in the middle so that's the selection we need to make.

8. Then click the OK button to insert your table parameters and the code into the edit page in the editor.

9. This particular editor doesn't include the code for a caption or much of anything else. So, we'll need to add a few codes if we want to do anything fancy. For our table, we do want the table centered so we need to add that command before the table commands start.

10. Type <CENTER> in the line before the table command.

11. Next you need to add a caption to the table. Type <CAPTION>Dogs—Man's Best Friend</CAPTION> after the <table align=Center width="60%" border=4 cellspacing=2> command the editor entered.

12. Now we need to enter the text for each of our rows and columns. At the end of the <TD align=Center valign=Middle> commands, type in the following:

```
<TD ALIGN="center"> Cocker Spaniel
<TD ALIGN="center"> Collie
<TR><TD ALIGN="center"> German Shepherd
<TD ALIGN="center"> Irish Setter
<TR><TD ALIGN="center"> Schnauser
<TD ALIGN="center"> Chihuahua
<TR><TD ALIGN="center"> Pekinese
<TD ALIGN="center"> Poodle
```

Be sure to remove all the <!— Table row:1, col:1 //—> in the edit page. Nothing will happen if you don't. They just take up space and could confuse you. They are only unnecessary prompts. Keep in mind, this prompt line is specific to this HTML Notes editor. The other editors won't have this prompt. However, they may have one of their own.

13. Let's preview it to see how it's going to look on our page. Click on the preview icon. See Figure 8.9 for an example of the preview of this table we've made so far.

We have a simple table ready for us to add some extras to it. In the next few steps we'll add background color, text color, and link the cells.

Figure 8.9 *Preview of the Dog Table.*

14. To add background color we need to add the command in this particular editor because it doesn't do it for us. The command is BGCOLOR="#hexcode". We add this code after the initial code to start the table.

15. We want our background color to be aqua so we need to enter that code, which is 00FFFF. I type BGCOLOR="#00FFFF" after the CELLSPACING figure.

16. To add color to the text you need to add the command to change the font color. That HTML command is <FONT COLOR="#hex code">Text</FONT>. Because our text is already there, we just need to add this command around the text.

17. The program has a tool to let us insert this code so all we need to do is highlight the text and click on the icon to make it happen.

18. Then select the color you want for the text and the text size if you want to change that also. Let's choose red for all the text.

YOU'LL THANK YOURSELF LATER

The easiest and fastest way to enter the same element repeatedly is to type it once and then copy and paste it into the repeat areas.

19. You'll also want to set your font size here. To get a decent sized font, select 3 from the font size drop-down menu.

We've added quite a bit of code to this page for this table. Let's take a look at how it should look so far.

```
<CENTER>
<table align=Center width="60%" border=4
cellspacing=2 BGCOLOR="#00FFFF">
<CAPTION>Dogs - Man's Best Friend</CAPTION>
<tr>
<TD align=Center valign=Middle><font face="Times
New Roman" color="Red" size=3>Cocker
Spaniel</font>
</td>
<TD align=Center valign=Middle><font face="Times
New Roman" color="Red" size=3>Collie</font>
</td>
<tr>
<TD align=Center valign=Middle><font face="Times
New Roman" color="Red" size=3>German
Shepherd</font>
  </td>
<TD align=Center valign=Middle><font face="Times
New Roman" color="Red" size=3>Irish Setter</font>
  </td>
 <tr>
  <TD align=Center valign=Middle><font
face="Times New Roman" color="Red"
size=3>Schnauser</font>
  </td>
  <TD align=Center valign=Middle><font
face="Times New Roman" color="Red"
size=3>Chihuahua</font>
  </td>
 <tr>
  <TD align=Center valign=Middle><font
face="Times New Roman" color="Red"
size=3>Pekinese</font>
  </td>
  <TD align=Center valign=Middle><font
face="Times New Roman" color="Red"
size=3>Poodle</font>
  </td>
</tr>
</table>
```

Lastly, we want to make links out of these items in our table.

20. Highlight the text you want to make your link.

21. Then click on the link icon in the editor.

22. A dialog box appears that asks you to type in the link address and a name for the link. Enter the link address and type the name you want to appear in your table. For this exercise, we're going to make Collies a link. Therefore, we need to type an address for the link. Let's use the fictitious address of http://www.collies.com. Then we need to enter the name for this link, so type Collies.

23. When you're done, click on the OK button. The link is now incorporated into your table.

24. Now, take a look at what you created. Click on the Preview icon.

See Figure 8.10 for an example of how the code should look for setting up this table with background color, text color, and links. Yours should look similar to this. See Figure 8.11 for an example of how the table will appear on your page.

That's it! That's all there is to it. You've now mastered creating tables for your site.

QUICK ⬛ PAINLESS

If you've already set up your table and entered the text for the cells, you'll need to reenter that information into the Text box in the dialog box for creating a link. The program erases what you originally typed and insert whatever you type in the Text box.

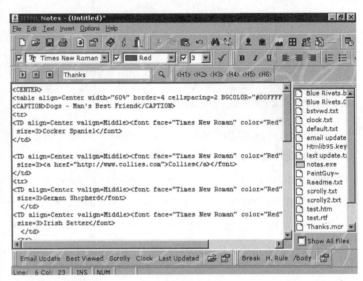

Figure 8.10 *HTML Notes HTML editor showing the codes for a table configuration.*

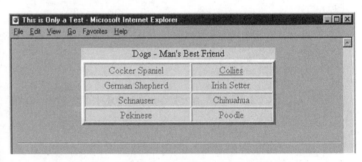

Figure 8.11 *Preview view of the table created in the HTML Notes editor.*

With all the steps you've learned in this chapter, you can now create a table to install almost any effect you want in your site. You can create a calendar, links, an image in a table format, and many other elements. Whatever your heart desires is now just a few clicks away when you use an HTML editor.

You've learned how to create a table. You deserve a pat on the back! You should celebrate this victory. Because we've talked about tables here, go get yourself a big glass of milk and some Oreos and sit at your table dipping Oreos in the milk and gloating in your success!

Now that you've mastered tables, lists will be no match for you. Let's move on to the next chapter and see how easy it is to create bulleted or numbered lists in our pages.

Razzle, Dazzle 'Em

Images and other graphics are some of the elements that jazz up a site and make it more interesting. They give the eye something pleasing to look at.

Graphics can make your site or they can detract from it. They can be a hindrance to you and your visitors in both time and design. Therefore, you need to use them wisely.

Pictures, icons, and other graphics are what have made the Web so popular. So you don't want to ignore them altogether. Armed with the proper techniques, you can build a site that is pleasing to you and your visitors without chasing them away.

Web sites are very much like magazines. They have pages, which contain text and pictures. Your job is to make your magazine as graphically enhanced and informative as possible.

There are a number of ways you can use graphics in your site. You can use clip art to illustrate points in your text. Images make great logos and links to other pages. Many personal sites include images of the family or pets to show off the owner's pride for their loved ones.

Business sites use images to display their products or to illustrate the services they have to offer. They also use them for product or company recognition.

As you've seen on sites when you surf the Web, there are many ways graphics are used in pages. But before you can begin using them, you need a general understanding of the various graphic formats.

WHAT HAVE WE HERE? IMAGE FORMATS

Images for your computer can be saved or created in a few different formats. The pictures you see on Web sites generally come in one of three formats—GIF, JPEG, or BMP.

Each of these are the suffix that follows the name of the image. For instance, redbox.gif, redbox.jpeg or redbox.jpg, or redbox.bmp.

The GIF format is an acronym for Graphics Interchange Format. Compuserve invented it. GIFs are simple formats using a series of colored elements called pixels that line up to make the picture.

JPEG stands for Join Photographic Equipment Group, which is the group who invented it. It is a compressed format. It compresses the image down while it's being stored saving hard drive space.

The BMP format stands for bitmap. These type of images tend to be larger than their GIF or JPEG counterparts. You'll see fewer of these used on sites because of their larger size.

A COMPLETE WASTE OF TIME

Don't scan or use images from published works that aren't in the public domain. You'll be inviting trouble with the copyright laws otherwise.

These formats are important when you're conscious of the size of the graphics you want to put on your site. Size affects the speed of loading pages.

Size can affect graphics and pages in two ways. Of course, there's the time it takes them to load. Then there's how they appear on the page. A graphic that's too large makes the visitor have to scroll to view it all.

To keep download time to a minimum, try not to use images larger than 20 to 50 kilobytes. If you do want to use a large graphic that spans the width of your page, make sure it's not more than 530 pixels wide. You can also have a graphic span down the page. However, if you do, keep it within a screen or two in length. People don't like to scroll.

With graphics on Web pages, smaller is better, especially on your front door or home page. First time you've heard that, huh? There are a few ways you can create small graphic files. One way is to make *thumbnails* of larger graphics. A thumbnail is a smaller copy of a large image. In Web pages, they're generally used as links to the larger picture. Another is to convert bitmaps or JPEGs into GIF files. Either of these techniques requires the use of an image program such as Adobe's GIF Export Filter or PhotoShop Pro.

WHO GOES THERE? PLACING IMAGES ON YOUR PAGES

When you use images in your HTML pages, you are also using special tags to tell the program how you want those images formatted. After you decide what images

you are going to use, you want to decide where to put them in your pages. Then you want to tell the program where you want your text to go around the image. Each of these decisions requires tags to instruct the program of your formatting desires.

Following are the basic image tags you use.

<IMG SRC="file name"> Image tag—This tag tells the program to insert a graphic file in between the angle brackets. You need to type in the name and location of the file between the brackets. For example, <IMG SRC="cat.gif">.

The tag to insert images breaks down as follows:

- IMG—the image command
- SRC—the source command for the location of the image in your files
- File—the file path, directory, and name: for instance, C:/1-4-All/images/cat.jpeg

When using graphics in your pages, you need and want to be able to choose how and where they appear on the page. You also want to allow for how the text appears in relation to those images. You want the ability to align your text and graphics on your pages.

If you use images and text together, you need to place a paragraph <P> tag before the image. You need to make sure the image and text that follows falls under the same paragraph tag.

There is a special code that lets you accomplish this. The code is: <IMG SRC=file name ALIGN="top, right, left, bottom">. This code tells the program to align your graphic in a certain way within a paragraph. For example, if you want to set your figure to the left (and consequently wrap your text around the right side of the image) you would type <IMG SRC="cat.jpeg" ALIGN="left">. The left, right, and center alignment commands align the picture on the page. The top, bottom, and middle commands align the text around the image. If you use the top command, the text starts at the top of the image for one line and then continues on the next line after the image. For middle it starts at the middle (to the side) of the image for one line and continues on the next line after the image. The bottom command works best for images because the text appears to flow unbroken. See Figure 9.1 for an example of a Web page with this graphic inserted using left alignment.

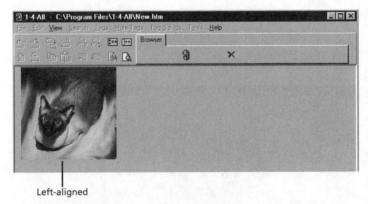

Left-aligned

Figure 9.1 *Preview of an image inserted into a page using the image tags with alignment specifications (to the left).*

When you don't specify how you want the image aligned in a paragraph (which decides the text flow), by

Be sure to preview your pages in different browsers to make sure your images and text are aligned the way you intend them. Different browsers have different screen widths and move elements in your pages around to fit their screens. If this happens you'll have to adjust your images to fit those browsers.

default the program aligns text at the bottom of the graphic. You never use this ALIGN code by itself. You use it with the IMG code.

That takes care of how the text wraps around the graphic. Now let's see about aligning the image on the page. After the IMG command, you need to enter an ALIGN command. If you want the image placed to the right of the page, you need to indicate that in this ALIGN command. If you want it centered, you have to place the <CENTER></CENTER> commands before and after the IMG command. The default is for the image to be aligned flush left. Therefore, the code would look like this if we wanted the image to be centered and the text to start at the top of the image:

```
<CENTER>
<IMG SRC="cat.jpeg" ALIGN="top">Siamese Cat
</CENTER>
```

See Figure 9.2 for an example of how this code looks in a Web page.

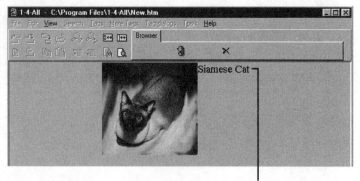

Text aligned at top of image

Figure 9.2 *Preview of image inserted aligned to the center with text at the top.*

When you're placing images on your site, remember those people who can't view graphics. For those with text-only browsers such as Lynx (or with browsers with auto-load images turned off), or those who are sight impaired, you need to provide text alternatives to your graphics.

This involves using text to inform the visitor about what he or she is not seeing. The code for this is ALT="text". You replace the word text in this sequence with the description. Therefore, our cat image with this text alternative added would have a source code of: <IMG SRC="cat.jpeg" ALT="picture of a siamese cat" ALIGN="top">Siamese Cat.

Providing this text alternative to graphics enables all users the ability to fully experience and participate in your site, no matter what their limitations. Adding this alternative has no effect on those visitors using a graphical interface browser.

Once you get your images inserted, you can start playing around with them and manipulating them to perform in specific ways for you. Think of it as training your images like you train a dog. Next, we're going to learn how to turn an image into a hyperlink, remove hyperlink borders, and change image sizes. Then, after we've mastered these, we'll work on some more complicated image manipulations, such as creating faster-loading images, creating low-resolution images, creating transparent images, and creating thumbnail images.

YOU'LL THANK YOURSELF LATER

Any images you want to use on your site must be in separate files. They can't be part of other files or documents, such as part of word processor files.

TRAINING THE DOG: MANIPULATING IMAGES

You can link images just like you link text. It's just a matter of inserting the hyperlink codes around the IMG command. So, if we want to make our cat image a link, here is what the code would look like:

```
<CENTER>
<A HREF="link address"><IMG SRC="C:/1-4-
All/images/cat.jpeg"></A>
</CENTER>
```

The <A HREF="link address"></A> is the command for a link. The A stands for Anchor and the HREF stands for Hypertext REFerence. This command simply means you're anchoring a hypertext reference to text or an image or in a page. (You can learn more about hyperlinks in Chapter 10.)

When you change an image to a hyperlink, a visitor can place his cursor over the image and see that it's an active link and where the link goes. Then when he clicks on the image, the linked page loads.

Making images linked places a blue border around them. To remove this border you need to add a command to the image command. The command you add is BORDER="0". You add this between the IMG and SRC tags. Therefore, our cat image command would look like this if we remove the border.

```
<A HREF="link address"><IMG BORDER="0" SRC="C:/1-4-
All/images/cat.jpeg"></A>
```

You can change the size of an image you place in your pages. But remember, images on your computer

QUICK 'n' PAINLESS

Be kind to your visitors. Keep images as small as possible. A 100K JPEG image can take up to a full minute to load if the visitor is using a 28.8Kbps modem.

aren't like the photographs you hold in your hands. Computer images are made up of a lot of colored dots called pixels. Therefore, the numbers referred to in this section are referring to these pixels.

With any image you use, you can denote it by the number of pixels it occupies in a space. For instance, the cat picture used in these examples is 173 x 162 pixels. I get this figure using a graphics program I have. If you don't have a graphics program that gives you the height and width in pixels, you'll just have to guess or you can try loading the picture in your browser. Sometimes the browsers will give you the pixels for the image in the title bar at the top of the browser window.

If you want to change the viewing size of a graphic on your site, you need to indicate the size you want it to be in the IMG SRC command. You add HEIGHT="number of pixels" WIDTH="number of pixels" between the IMG and SRC tags. So, if we want to reduce the size our cat picture a little, we can use this command. Let's reduce it by 10 pixels in both height and width. Therefore, our code would look like this:

```
<IMG HEIGHT="163" WIDTH="152" SRC="C:/1-4-
All/images/cat.jpeg">
```

See Figure 9.3 for an example of how this code affects the picture we've been using.

QUICK ●■● PAINLESS

One way you can determine the size of an image is to load your page in a browser. Select one of your images and right-click on it. From the pop-up menu, choose View This Image. The image loads to a page by itself. The pixel counts appear on this new page.

Whenever possible, use the GIF format. JPEGs are great if you're trying to save space; however, they aren't so great for those using computers with smaller memory capacities. They require much more memory to expand to their original size, which can cause the smaller machines to run out of memory and possibly crash their browser.

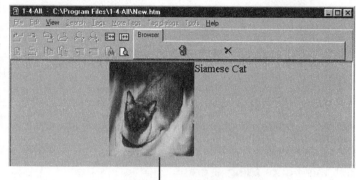

Image altered with HTML code

Figure 9.3 *Preview of the cat image reduced 10 pixels around.*

Notice there are striated lines running down the picture when viewed in the editor's preview mode. It appears almost normal in a browser. This happens when you try to manipulate images by changing their size. Making the picture larger can cause it to become blurry and distorted. You just have to play around until you find the right combination that leaves you with a nice smaller or larger picture. Each picture will react differently, so there's no sure-fire formula to use. And sometimes you just have to leave images as they are.

Changing the image's physical size in the code does *not* change its file size. If you want to change the actual file size, you'll need to do that in a graphics manipulation program such as PhotoShop Pro. If you have such a program, this is actually a better method to reduce an image's size.

Another way to reduce an image's file size is to reduce the resolution of the image. The standard screen resolution is 72 dpi (dot per inch). There is no real need to have a resolution higher than that.

OBEDIENCE SCHOOL: MORE ADVANCED IMAGE MANIPULATION

Since speed is so important in designing a site, it's helpful to know how you can make your images load faster. With this next technique you're not actually going to get your images or pages to load faster, you're only giving the impression that they're loading faster.

Fill in the Blanks

I know you've been to some sites where you have waited for what seemed like forever for their page to load. All the while, you sat staring at a blank page. That's very frustrating to a visitor and can cause them to give up and go elsewhere.

To prevent this from happening, you can cause your text to load and have boxes appear with text in them. This gives the impression that your page is loading much faster than it is. And it gives the visitor something to read while they wait for your images to appear.

Here's how you do this little trick. You add the HEIGHT, WIDTH, and ALT commands to the IMG SRC command. The whole command would look like this:

```
<IMG HEIGHT="number of pixels" WIDTH="number of
pixels" ALT="descriptive text" SRC="image.gif">
```

It appears to load faster because a box appears where the picture will be. The alternative text gives the

QUICK PAINLESS

When designing your pages, concentrate on content over flash. All the latest technology can make for a highly impressive site. But balancing a table and chair on your nose is impressive, too. However, too much gets old after awhile.

When creating image files, use clear naming conventions. For instance, smcat.gif and lgcat.gif, or bwcat.gif and clrcat.gif for black and white image and color image. This helps you find and place images quicker and easier.

visitor something to read while the image is loading. It also lets the visitor know a picture is on its way.

So, to take an example we've already been working with, if we want our cat picture page to appear to load faster, our command would look like this:

```
<IMG HEIGHT="173" WIDTH="162" ALT="Picture of a
Siamese cat" SRC="C:/1-4-All/images/cat.jpeg">
```

That was easy, wasn't it?

Monochrome

Another way to get images to load faster is to use the LOWSRC command. This command is very useful when you're using rather large graphics. Basically what you're doing is loading two images. You load a black and white image first, then the color image replaces the black and white image. The black and white image is the LOWSRC image. This is how the command looks:

```
<IMG HEIGHT="number of pixels" WIDTH="number of
pixels" ALT="descriptive text" SRC="image.gif" LOWS-
RC="image.gif">
```

For our cat image, the code would look like this:

```
<IMG HEIGHT="173" WIDTH="162" ALT="Picture of a
Siamese cat" SRC="C:/1-4-All/images/cat.jpeg" LOWS-
RC=bwcat.jpeg>.
```

Of course, you have to have a black and white copy of the image you want to use. You can use one of the graphics programs to make this copy.

Black and white graphics are much smaller in size; therefore, they load faster. This makes them a low source in the Web server's eyes. That's the reason for the command LOWSRC instead of LOWRES. It appears almost instantly. Then the color picture wipes over the top of it as it loads. Using the HEIGHT and WIDTH commands creates a box where the picture goes and, of course, the ALT command displays the descriptive alternative text while the graphics are loading and to those who aren't using a graphics viewer or browser.

You could use this command for all of your images. But you especially want to use it for your larger images.

Transparencies

Another method you can use with images is to make them transparent or make parts of them transparent. What this does is make it seem as though you can see through areas of a picture to the background. Transparent images seem to load faster. The visitor sees the background come in and then the image slides in over it, making it seem to the view that the image is loading much faster than it is.

The only type of images you can do this on are GIF format images. What you'll need to do is get a program that can convert a GIF to a transparent image. There are many programs; two of the best are PaintShop Pro and LView Pro.

Using one of these programs, you simply highlight the area in the photo you want to be transparent and save the image in a special format named GIF89a. It was given this name because the GIF format was standardized in 1989. The transparency was a secondary part of the list of standards, therefore the "a" in the format.

Once you have your transparent image, you simply treat it like any other image you want to place in your pages. Use the IMG SRC command to add it to your site. You can manipulate these images just like any other image.

Thumbnails

Another means to get images to load faster is to offer thumbnails of larger images. Thumbnails are just smaller versions of the larger pictures. There are two ways you can offer thumbnails in your pages. One is to offer two images and the other is to offer one image.

With the two images option, you offer a smaller version of the image that visitors click to see the larger version (which is a separate file). For the one-image option, you offer the same image as both the thumbnail and the larger image (manually sizing the thumbnail in HTML code).

The two-image offering is what you see most often on Web sites. Basically you have a thumbnail image (one file) linked to the larger image (a second file). The command is a link command paired with the IMG SRC command. It looks like this:

```
<A HREF="link image address"><IMG
SRC="image.gif"></A>
```

You can also add text to this to let the visitor know there is a larger picture. If we were to have a larger picture of our cat and we wanted to use the smaller picture as a thumbnail to point to the larger picture, our command might look like this:

```
<A HREF=cat2.JPG"><IMG SRC=" cat.jpg"
ALIGN="TOP"></A>Click here to see the bigger pic-
ture.
```

Remember that the link is going to be the address of the bigger picture. Unless you want your text to also be part of the link, add it after the closing Anchor tag.

The only problem with this technique is that it requires you to have two pictures to load. Otherwise, it's very easy to use.

If you prefer to only use one image as the thumbnail and the larger picture, you can. What you do is make the link to the same image as the thumbnail. You create the thumbnail in the HTML code by altering the HEIGHT and WIDTH size of the larger image. The command looks like this:

```
<A HREF="full size image address"><IMG HEIGHT="num-
ber of pixels" WIDTH="number of pixels"
SRC="image.gif"></A>.
```

Therefore, if we use the large cat picture and reduce the height and width in the command for the thumbnail, our command might look like this:

```
<A HREF="cat2.JPG"><IMG HEIGHT="150" WIDTH="130"
SRC="cat2.JPG" ALIGN="TOP"></A>Click here to see the
bigger picture.
```

Remember, when you start reducing the size of a picture in HTML, you're going to get some distortion. You have to decide if the distortion is worth the thumbnail.

If you want distortion-free smaller graphics, work with your images in a graphics manipulation program. In these programs you can alter the size of the picture to the size you want and then insert it into your page.

While you're using the photo manipulation program to alter the size of your graphics, you can use it to reduce the resolution of images. The resolution of an image can affect the file size and the download time of an image. Generally, an image doesn't need to be any higher than 72 dpi in resolution. Most graphic manipulation programs let you change the resolution of any image.

That wasn't so hard now, was it? It all looks much harder than it is. These techniques should give you a good start on adding images to your site. Of course, the easiest way to add these elements is to use an HTML editor.

LET YOUR WEB PAGE EDITOR DO IT FOR YOU

Any of the HTML editors you use insert the image tags automatically when you want to include images in your pages. Most of them have some kind of icon you can click on to insert the image. Some use a camera for the icon, while others use a picture as an icon.

Once you click on the image icon, the program generally gives you a dialog box. In this dialog box you enter the address for the image. Usually, the program gives you the option to browse through the files on your hard drive to locate the file. Then you simply double-click on the filename and it's inserted in the address line. See

Figure 9.4 for an example of the dialog box for the 1-4-All editor.

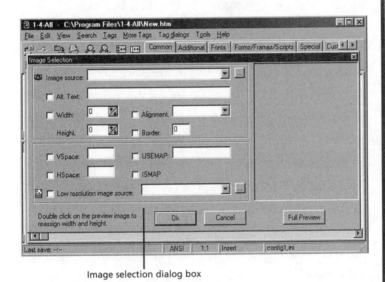

Image selection dialog box

Figure 9.4 *Insert Image dialog box for the 1-4-All HTML editor.*

Some of the editors let you set up other options through this dialog box. For instance, the 1-4-All editor lets you enter alternative text, set the text alignment, set a border width, indicate the height and width of an image, and give a low resolution image source. It also lets you preview how the image will appear.

If you want to create a link of an image, insert the image first, then highlight the whole image command and click on the link icon. A hyperlink dialog box pops up and you simply fill in the address box.

To perform any of the other techniques covered in this chapter, you'll have to enter the tags manually.

Editors are set up to handle the most basic of tasks. But once you insert the image into a page, it's fairly easy to add these other commands to the IMG SRC tags.

PROJECT

Images and graphics are the main ingredients that jazz up a Web site. This is the part of this book you were probably most interested in. So let's tackle adding the one-image thumbnail to our page. This one technique uses most of the elements covered in this chapter.

Begin by opening the HTML editor you want to use. I'll be using the Site Builder editor for this project. Remember that each editor works in its own way, so you'll need to check the help files and documentation for the editor you choose to become familiar with it.

1. Click on the Insert Image icon for the editor you're using.

2. In the dialog box you get, enter the address for the image you want to use. I am using the picture of the Siamese cat.

   You can use the browse function in the dialog box to locate the file on your hard drive. Then double-click the file once you locate it. The program inserts it into the Image Address line.

3. Type the alternative text you want for this picture in the Alternative Text box, if your editor has this option.

4. Leave the border width set at zero.

5. Indicate how you want the text to wrap around the image. I am choosing Top.

6. Since we're going to use this image as a thumbnail, we need to indicate the Height and Width for the image. Enter those numbers in pixels in the Height and Width boxes.

   I want to make my image 150 pixels in height and 125 pixels in width, which makes a nice small thumbnail. Therefore, I type those values in the two relevant boxes in the dialog box.

   See Figure 9.5 for an example of the Insert Image dialog box for the Site Builder editor. Notice in this dialog box, all the fields are filled in. This is similar to what your dialog box should look like.

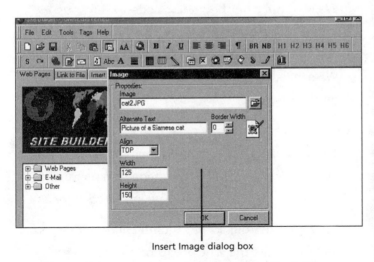

Insert Image dialog box

Figure 9.5 *Insert Image dialog box in the Site Builder editor with values entered.*

7. Click the OK button to insert the image into your page.

   See Figure 9.6 for an example of the code we just set up entered into our edit page.

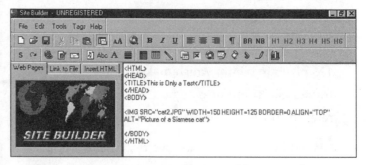

Figure 9.6 *Edit screen in the Site Builder HTML editor with the code to insert an image entered.*

We now have our beginning code to start our thumbnail and make it a link. As this code stands, the image will flush to the left margin of our page. We can leave it there or we can center the image on the page.

8. To center the image, we need to enter the code before and after the image command. Type <CEN-TER> in the line before the image command, and </CENTER> in the line after the image command.

9. Now it's time to link that thumbnail to our larger picture. Select the whole IMG command.

10. Click on the Link icon.

11. In the dialog box you get, enter the address for the image. You can again use the browse function to find this file.

12. Enter a description of the image in the Description or Text field.

    For the Site Builder editor, I need to reenter the image command in this Description field. Otherwise my IMG command is replaced by the text I enter.

13. Click the OK button to insert the hyperlink around the image command.

14. Our image is now a thumbnail linked to the larger picture. Let's go take a look at it. Click on the Preview option.

See Figure 9.7 for an example of how the thumbnail looks in the page, and Figure 9.8 for an example of how the larger picture looks.

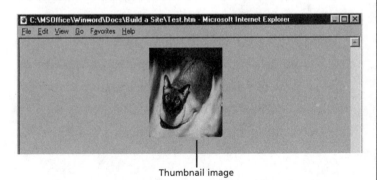

Thumbnail image

Figure 9.7 *View in a browser of the thumbnail linking image.*

What a great student you are! The very best! You deserve a break now. Put your feet up and tune into a great movie on the television.

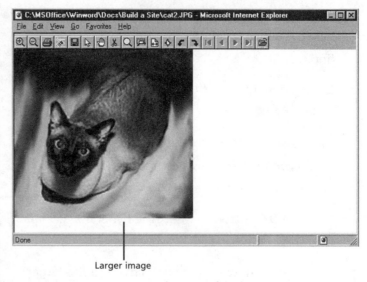

Larger image

Figure 9.8   *View in a browser of the larger image.*

While images are what visitors probably enjoy the most when they surf the Web, they can be intimidating. The techniques you learned in this chapter should alleviate some of the tension surrounding using images in your site.

Using the steps and commands covered in this chapter, it should be easy for you to add almost any kind of image to your site and pages. In this chapter, you got a short lesson on linking. The next chapter gives you even more ammunition to use links effectively in your site.

Chapter ten

Pass the Baton

Hyperlinks are the other element that makes the Web so dynamic. These links are why it was created in the first place. They make sharing information so much easier.

Links help visitors navigate through your site or lead them to other sites related to yours. Why would you want to lead visitors out of your site? I've been giving you ways to keep visitors at your site throughout this book.

You don't—except to lead them to information that backs up the information on your site. Leading them to related sites or sites with authoritative information provides a service to your visitors. It tells them you care about them and are willing to help them.

Local links, links to areas or pages within your site, also provide a service to your visitors. These type of links make it easier for them to find the information they want.

When you help your visitors, they are more likely to return to you. So leading them away can also lead them back—especially if the other sites you link to link back to you.

For local links, make sure you create separate files for each segment of content. Then make sure the link anchors reference these files correctly. For instance, if you have a large document with various segments broken up by headings and you want to link to each of those segments, you can place each segment into a separate file. This chapter could be broken into segments by each heading with a file for each heading.

FOLLOW THE YELLOW BRICK ROAD

Hyperlinks are specially coded linking commands that tell the program to take you to or load another file for you to view. In HTML documents, these links are usually highlighted and underlined. When you click on these hyperlinks, the new page or file is loaded for you. These links can either be areas or pages within your Web presence or other pages on the World Wide Web.

To create these hyperlinks, you use special tags called *anchors*. Anchors are paired tags. Following are the hyperlink tags that are used in your pages and how they work.

- <A HREF="URL">Hyperlinked text</A>—Hyperlinks to another page on the Web. When typing this link you would insert the address of the page you want to link to after the HREF=. For example: <A HREF="http://www.swbell.com/"></A>.

- <A HREF="directory/file.ext">Linked Text</A>—Hyperlinks to a file within your pages. Here you would insert the file name and location for the file to which you are linking. Example: <A HREF="c:/windows/word/resume.doc"dbase.msoffice>Linked text</A>.

You can use these anchor tags to link to any documents, files, or pages you would like. You can even use them to create hyperlinks of images. (Image hyperlinks are discussed in more detail in Chapter 9.)

You want to include hyperlinks in your pages. They are a way to connect your visitors to other pages on the

Web that are related to your site's subject matter and to direct them to other related interesting material either within your pages or on other pages.

One way you can link to other pages or other sites is to use images or logos. Several sites use this technique. It's an effective and interesting method for providing links. See Figure 10.1 for an example of a site that uses images as links.

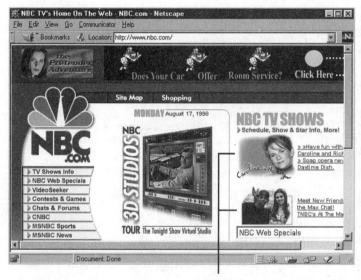

Image as links

Figure 10.1 *NBC site with images as links to other pages within its site. You can click on any of the images to link to another document.*

Getting More Complicated: Link Buttons

After you have these hyperlinks established in your pages, you can enhance them by creating a *link button*.

A link button is a button on your page that opens another site or page when the visitor clicks on it. You can manipulate those buttons by lining them up to get a more pleasing or varied design.

It's fairly easy to make a link button with your own wording. Using link buttons brightens up your pages and gives you a nice alternative to the normal format of underlined blue words indicating links. Link buttons also look more professional.

To create a link button use a FORM command. Creating forms is covered in more detail in Chapter 11. But for the purpose of creating a link button, we'll use part of the FORM command. The command looks like this:

```
<FORM METHOD="LINK" ACTION="address">
<INPUT TYPE="Submit" VALUE="Text you want to appear
on button">
</FORM>.
```

The following is what each of these tags mean and what they do:

- FORM—Lets the program know a form item is being inserted. This is a paired tag, therefore you'll need the closing </FORM> tag.

- METHOD—Tells the program how to handle the form command; for instance, in this case you're making a link.

- ACTION—Indicates what connection you want to make. For the link buttons, this would be the linking address. Make sure you use the full address.

YOU'LL THANK YOURSELF LATER

When inserting addresses for links, make sure you type them correctly. Always use forward slashes (/) for subdirectory references.

The second command creates and places the button on the page. This is the INPUT command. Following is how this INPUT command breaks down and what it does:

- INPUT TYPE—Indicates what text you want on the input. Use "Submit" which tells that you are submitting a link. The FORM command is looking for a link.

- VALUE—Indicates the wording you want to appear on the button.

Therefore, we could make a clickable button like this:

```
<FORM METHOD="LINK" ACTION="http://www.swbell.net">
<INPUT TYPE="Submit" VALUE="Clickable Button">
</FORM>
```

See Figure 10.2 for an example of how this Link button looks in a page.

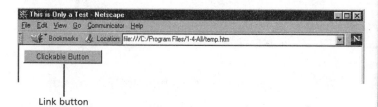

Link button

Figure 10.2 *Browser view of clickable button.*

There is one downfall to using this link button. The command places a question mark after the address you use as the link. To eliminate the problem of a browser reading the address as bad because of that question mark, place a forward slash mark at the end of the link to address in the command.

This moves the question mark placement to after that slash and prevents the browser from misinterpreting

it. There is no way to totally eliminate this question mark from appearing in the address.

Now that we've learned how to create these little jewels, we can move on to learn how to line them up in a page. To accomplish this, you need to separate the buttons. What you want to do is make it so the other buttons don't know that other buttons are around them on the same page.

This sounds a little complicated, but it's basically a simple process. The way you separate these buttons is by placing them in a table. You can review how to create tables in Chapter 8. Here is how the command looks:

```
<TABLE BORDER="number of pixels">
<TD><FORM METHOD="LINK" ACTION="link address">
<INPUT TYPE="Submit" VALUE="Text">
</FORM>
<TD><FORM METHOD="LINK" ACTION="link address">
<INPUT TYPE="Submit" VALUE="Text">
</FORM>
(and so on for each button)
</TABLE>
```

This gives you link buttons that are side by side. See Figure 10.3 for an example of how these buttons appear in a page.

With a few additions to this TABLE/FORM command you can make the buttons run up and down rather than side-by-side. The commands you add are the <TR> and ALIGN="alignment" commands. To line these link buttons running down a page, the commands would look like this:

```
<TABLE BORDER="number of pixels">
<TD ALIGN="alignment"><FORM METHOD="LINK"
ACTION="link address">
<INPUT TYPE="Submit" VALUE="Text">
</FORM>
```

A COMPLETE WASTE OF TIME

One thing you don't want to do with links is use "click here" or "here". This is passé. Instead, use a keyword from your text. For instance, "you can view my resume." Resume would be the linking word. You can use this technique for both local and external links.

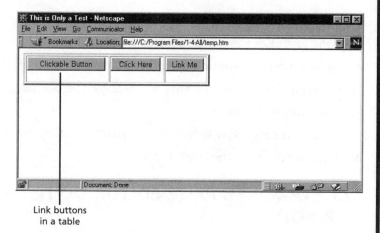

Link buttons
in a table

Figure 10.3 *Browser view of side-by-side link buttons created using a table.*

```
<TD ALIGN="alignment"><FORM METHOD="LINK"
ACTION="link address">
<INPUT TYPE="Submit" VALUE="Text">
</FORM>
<TR>
(and so on for each button)
</TABLE>
```

See Figure 10.4 for an example of how these link buttons now appear running down the page.

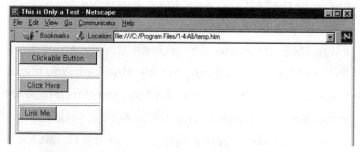

Figure 10.4 *Browser view of link buttons arranged to run down a page using a table format.*

Using the TABLE commands you can line up your link buttons just about any way that you want. The table is really just there to separate the buttons from each other, however, it does make it easier to arrange the buttons the way you want them.

That was easy! Now let's make it easier by letting our Web page editor do the work for us.

LET YOUR WEB PAGE EDITOR DO IT FOR YOU

Any time you want to add a hyperlink into your pages or make an image a hyperlink, HTML editors make it easy for you. You click on the Hyperlink icon and type in the address to which you want to link and any text you want to appear as the link. It's that simple.

If you already have the text entered on the page, you can highlight the text and then click on the Hyperlink icon. In the dialog box that appears, you should only have to type the address to which to link. However, some HTML editors expect you to retype this information even if you highlight the text you want to appear as the linked text.

When you want to link images, you highlight the entire IMG command and click on the Hyperlink icon. Then proceed as you would for any other link. You might want to review Chapter 9 to find out the different ways you can manage images and link images in your site.

Adding links to your pages is one of the easiest techniques you can perform using an HTML editor. The biggest obstacle you'll run up against is typing the address correctly.

QUICK ● PAINLESS

Be sure to choose anchor reference words that fit into the context of your content. In other words, the text you use for your links should relate to the content of your reference or of the information in your site.

PROJECT

Because adding links to your pages is so simple, we're going to do something a little more involved. We're going to create a link button. Then we're going to arrange several link buttons to run down a page. The first thing you need to do is open the Web page editor you want to use. For this project I'll be using the HTML Notes editor.

Remember that not all editors handle these techniques the same way. Be sure to adjust these instructions for the editor you're using. Because this is a FORM command and not a LINK command, you have to start with the FORM command.

1. Click on the Form icon if your editor offers one. HTML Notes does have a form generator. It gives me a Form dialog box to assist in setting up a form.

2. Select the Form type you want to use. This is the information that follows the METHOD tag. Let's select POST or the equivalent for your editor. Because there is no LINK option in these editors, you have to replace the METHOD tag they furnish with LINK. We'll change this after the command is entered in our editor.

3. Click on the Insert button.

4. Go to the edit page and replace POST with LINK.

5. Then type ACTION="http://www.swbell.com/" following "LINK" and a space.

6. Next we need to indicate how we want the Input to function. Click the Input tab, or the equivalent your editor has. Select Submit from the choices.

   If your editor doesn't offer this option, you'll have to hand type the INPUT command. Type <INPUT TYPE="Submit" VALUE="Click Me">.

7. Space down a line and type </FORM> to close the link button form.

   You've now made a link button. Go take a look at it. Click on the Preview icon.

   Now that you've mastered creating a link button, let's arrange a few to run down a page.

8. Scroll up to the line before the start of this FORM command you used to create the link button.

9. Type <TABLE BORDER="3">.

10. On the line with the FORM command and before it begins, type <TD ALIGN="left">.

11. Space down one line after the </FORM> tag and type <TR>.

12. Repeat step 10 and then continue.

13. Copy and paste the whole FORM command in this line.

14. Replace the address with a new address—use http://www.cbs.com/.

15. Repeat step 11.

16. Repeat steps 12 through 14. Use http://www. prevue.com/ as the address for this second button. Make sure you have the <TR> command following the end of each FORM ending tag.

17. After the last </FORM> tag, space down a line and type </TABLE>.

You have now created several link buttons and arranged them to run down the left-hand side of the page. Go take a look at what you did. Click on the Preview icon. See Figure 10.5 for an example of how these link buttons appear on the page, and Figure 10.6 for an example of how the code should look in your editor.

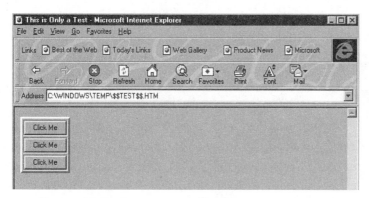

Figure 10.5 *Browser view of link buttons project.*

Linking is what the Web is all about. In this chapter, you've learned how you can spice up your links and make your pages look more attractive.

You now have enough information to create just about any kind of link on your site, from normal links, to image links, to link buttons. Armed with what you've learned so far, you're now ready to tackle some of the more advanced techniques used in Web sites—video, sound, and other elements.

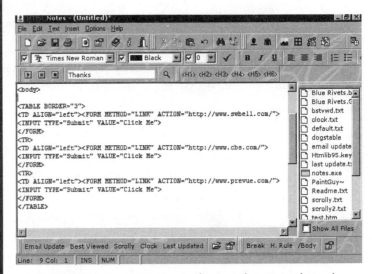

Figure 10.6 *HTML Notes edit page showing code used to create the link buttons lined up down the page.*

Chapter eleven

Hear the Roar,
Video at Five

There are many different elements you can add to your pages to jazz them up. Most of these elements require a little more effort and are more technically involved than what we've covered so far.

As part of building your Web site, you may want to add some of the more advanced features to your pages, such as:

- hidden comments
- time stamps
- marquees
- animated GIFs
- forms
- frames
- audio
- video
- chat

We will be covering these elements only as an overview in this chapter and book. The codes and commands are included so you can play around with them. These are some of the more advanced elements you can add to your site and require much more than is available for the scope of this book. If you want or need more information on these elements, there are many sites and books where you can find that information and help. Some of these will be included in the back matter of this book.

I'VE GOT A SECRET

There may be times when you want to put *hidden comments* into your pages. These may be comments to yourself or, as some sites are doing, to sway search results in their favor, packing sites with keywords. Several sites on the Web have learned that if they pack their pages with keywords that are commonly searched for by search engines, they can increase the chances of their pages appearing in the first few results on a results return page. They hide these packed terms within their pages.

You want some hidden keywords to help search engines find you, but anything over a couple of lines is too much. Packing a site involves a half page or more of these hidden keywords.

Your editor can view these hidden comments, but not from a Web browser. However, if someone chooses to view the source code, they can then see any hidden comments.

There are two ways you can hide comments in your

pages. One is with the COMMENT command and the other is with what is called a *META tag*. The META tag is a tag the program and server read, acknowledge but hide the text included in it. In this area you put keywords that search engines use to locate pages. These keywords would be words relevant to the purpose of your site. For instance, if your site's purpose was to offer computers for sale, your META tag would include the keywords computers, sale, discount, IBM, Macs, ComPaqs, and so forth.

To add hidden comments to your pages, you need to select where you want to insert your comments in your page. For the META tag, type comments you want to pack in the first section of the page, right after the title. For comments to yourself, just add them where you need them. For instance, you might add a comment at the end of a page to remind yourself to revise the date you update your site.

When you want to add a hidden comment, type the following command:

```
<!--Your Text Here-->.
```

For META comments use this command:

```
<META NAME="DESCRIPTION" CONTENT="Your Text here">
<META NAME="GENERATOR" CONTENT="name of software">
```

The META NAME="DESCRIPTION" in these meta tags is for placing your keywords. The META NAME="GENERATOR" is to show the software you use to create your pages. These tags should be placed between the HEAD tags and after the TITLE tag.

Most of the HTML editors have an icon or command you can click on to insert hidden comments. Some offer

YOU'LL THANK YOURSELF LATER

Although packing your site with comments sounds appealing, it's not advisable to do this. Many of the search engines are wise to this tactic and are devising ways around this. Some are even denying acceptance to their search engines' reporting if they find you are packing your pages.

the META tag as part of the edit page. In this case, you type your keywords over any the editor has placed in the command or insert keywords in the appropriate space.

If you wanted to place a reminder in your page to change the date in the last updated area, the code would look like this:

```
<!--Don't forget to update the timestamp area-->
```

When you want to add META tag keywords to your site that provide writing services, the command looks like this:

```
<META NAME="GENERATOR" CONTENT="writing, resumes,
ghost writing, business writing, technical writing,
books">
```

These two commands are pretty straightforward and simple to use. Use the hidden comments to make notes to yourself and use the META tag to help search engines find you and put you higher up on the hierarchy.

ANYONE GOT THE TIME?

Timestamps tell your visitors when your page was last updated. It lets them know if there's going to be new information or if they can just surf on to another site. It also lets them know how current the information is if they're doing research and using your site.

You can get a fancy script to automatically change the timestamp date for you each time you edit your pages. Or you can simply use two hidden comment commands and place the date between them. This version of the TIMESTAMP command would look like this:

```
<!--Comment-->Date<!--Comment-- >.
```

QUICK ☺ PAINLESS

Timestamps aren't necessary in a page. They merely provide added value to your visitors. At a glance, they can tell how current your site is and if there's any new information they need to check out.

Therefore, the TIMESTAMP command would look like this in your edit page:

```
<!--Arachnaphilia editor-->Last updated August 31,
1998<!--Arachnaphilia editor-->
```

The text within the <!-- -- > is in the comment tag and doesn't display on the page. The text between the two comment tags is what displays in the page.

See Figure 11.1 for an example of the Timestamp inserted in a page.

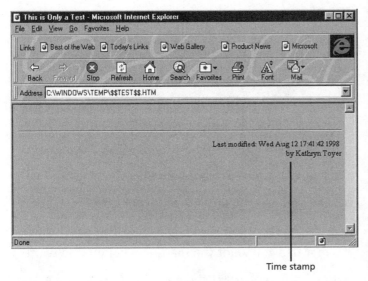

Time stamp

Figure 11.1 *Preview of a scripted timestamp inserted in a page.*

That's all there is to it. Then you enter the date you updated your pages when you edit them. Or you can just type "Last Updated" and the date at the end of the page. Then you would need to change the date manually each time you update your pages.

When the HTML editor you use offers this Timestamp as an option, click on the icon that is usually represented by a clock. Then enter the date, if that is what is required. Some editors like HTML Notes place a script in the page, therefore, you don't need to do anything once you add the Timestamp to the page.

THIS SPACE FOR RENT

Marquees are areas of scrolling or animated text. They are useful in drawing the visitor's attention to an important area.

When using the MARQUEE command you are given several options to direct the way you want your marquee to look. These include:

- the text you want to put in the marquee
- the direction you want the text to move; left or right
- the type of motion used to animate the marquee; scroll, slide, or alternate
- how you want it aligned with your other text; top, middle, or bottom
- what size you want the marquee; height and width
- how often you want the marquee to repeat the text you include; loops
- the background color for your marquee

The command for a marquee would look like this:

```
<MARQUEE ALIGN="alignment" HEIGHT="in pixels"
WIDTH="in pixels" BGCOLOR="hex code"
BEHAVIOR="motion" DIRECTION="direction to scroll"
LOOP="number or infinite>Text to scroll</MARQUEE>
```

YOU'LL THANK YOURSELF LATER

Be careful using marquees in your home page. Remember you don't want to overwhelm your visitors with too much input too fast. This element might serve you better on a secondary page.

The height is pretty much up to you to determine. It's how tall in pixels you want the marquee to be. The width is a little tricky. You might have to play around with it until you get it right, especially if you're using the slide option. For the text to slide the width has to be at least equal to the length of the message.

Alternate for the motion means that the text will scroll from left to right within the marquee area. Because these are moving targets, an example wouldn't do it justice.

If you wanted a scrolling marquee that read "Check our specials for today" with the alignment to the left, and a background color of yellow, the code would look like this:

```
<MARQUEE ALIGN="left" HEIGHT="3" WIDTH="200"
BGCOLOR="FFFF00" BEHAVIOR="scroll" DIRECTION="
alternate" LOOP="infinite">Check our specials
today</MARQUEE>
```

Another option is to select a percentage of the screen on which you want the marquee to run and use a shorter command that eliminates everything but the MARQUEE command, SCROLLDELAY, and BEHAVIOR. This command would look like this:

```
<MARQUEE WIDTH="percentage" SCROLLDELAY="loops"
BEHAVIOR=ALTERNATE>Text to scoll</MARQUEE>
```

If you wanted to use the other MARQUEE command to create a marquee announcing your specials to run across 50% of the page, the command would look like this:

```
<MARQUEE WIDTH="50%" SCROLLDELAY="0" BEHAVIOR=
ALTERNATE>Check our specials today</MARQUEE>
```

A COMPLETE WASTE OF TIME

Avoid using a scrolling marquee or text in the status bar. This only slows down the loading of your site, which could cause you to lose your visitors.

QUICK PAINLESS

Some browsers can't display marquees. Not to worry though. The visitor will still see your text.

IF YOU'RE SO
INCLINED

You can find animation GIFs at the following sites:

Gif Animations—
web2.airmail.net/
nicktg/moving

Tater Hollow—
www.otsego.net/thg/
index.htm

Mickey's Collection—
www.geocities.com/SoHo/
1085

When using your HTML editor, in the page where you want the marquee to appear, select the area in which you want it to appear. Then click on the MARQUEE command or icon. A dialog box appears that asks for specific information about how you want the marquee to appear and function. Fill in these boxes using the guidelines covered in the previous section, then test it to make sure it's working the way you want it to.

'TOON TOWN

Animation simply is a moving image. What happens is the browser places one GIF after another into the same space.

There are several reasons why you would want to use them in your pages. One is when you can't fit all your information in a single graphic. Another is if you want to send your visitors two or more different messages in a limited space. And of course, you can use them strictly for their entertainment value.

Using animation in your site gets your visitors involved in your site and gives them the feeling that they're doing something more than just reading a page. However, you want to be careful not to overuse animation.

Animation is one element you want to limit using on your home page. After a visitor gets beyond your front door page and becomes involved in your site, animation can be attractive.

You should avoid gratuitous animated GIFs such as send email animations, animated lists, and animated bullets. These types of animations are more or less just gimmicks and they slow down the download time for your pages.

To add animations to your Web site, you first need an extra program. You need a program that makes animations out of GIF format images. One such program is called the GIF Construction Set for Windows or Windows 95, depending on which operating system you use. Of course you can use any GIF animation program you prefer. You'll also need images to work with.

What you're doing when creating animations is creating small movies, frame by frame. For the animation to work, all the frames must be the same size and all the images must be in the same format and at the same color level.

After you have selected the images you want to animate, use the GIF Construction Set to convert them to animations. The program has documentation and excellent help files to assist you in this. The easiest way to add animation to your pages is to use animation files someone else has already created.

After you create an animation file, you can place it on your page. The code for this is the same as placing a normal image file. The command is: <IMG SRC="animation.gif">. Creating an animation is a process that involves several steps of saving frames of motion. If you've ever seen a flip book, it's the same process. Each frame is like each page in the flip book. When you're done, you have one image file that has motion.

Because adding animation is the same as adding a normal image to your site, the steps in an HTML editor are the same. The editors all have an icon or command to insert images into your pages quickly and easily. Click on this icon to insert the IMG SRC command and then select the animation file you want to insert.

Sometimes the animation appears to work when you preview the page in an editor but doesn't work on the actual page. In that case you'll need to make sure that the animation file and all the images you used to create it, if you used more than one image, are included when you hang your page. We'll tell you more about this in Chapter 12.

Animated GIFs are designed so that most visitors to your site can view them. They won't need extra plug-ins or other add-on tools. They don't require any special configuration or extra resources of a Web server. The server just sees it as another image file.

If you want to learn more about animations, look in the section at the end of this book titled "If You Really Want More, Read These." An example that comes to mind for animation is the "flaming logo" and the "spinning logo" you see on the IBM commercials. Those are the kind of things you can do with animation.

PLEASE FILL OUT THIS FORM

We fill out forms almost every day of our lives. When we go to the doctor, we fill out a form about our medical history. When we enroll in a class at the local college, we fill out a form. Almost everything we do these days requires us to fill out some sort of form. We fill out surveys by the dozen.

Forms have become a way of life for us. Sometimes they're fun to fill out and sometimes they're merely tedious.

You can add forms to your Web site. Basically, a form does what email does. It sends information to you. The visitor merely provides that information.

Let's begin by learning how to create a basic form. With forms you have several ways you can get visitors to give you information. One is to use text boxes to let the person enter information in their own words. Another is to provide choices with check boxes or radio buttons the person clicks on to make a choice. And, lastly, you can offer a pop-up box to let the visitor make a choice from. To create a basic form you need to start with this command:

```
<FORM METHOD="POST" ACTION="mailto:your email
address"></FORM>.
```

This command does three things. First it tells the program to start a FORM. Then it tells the program how to deal with the form—to POST it. And lastly it tells the program to email the data from the form to you in the ACTION part of the command.

Now that the form is started, the program is going to look for one of several form styles to deal with. There are five that are used most often in forms. These are:

- TEXT—A text box that allows one line of text.

- TEXT AREA—A larger text box that allows the visitor more room to enter text.

- RADIO BUTTON—Places an active circle on a page and allows a visitor to use his mouse to click on it to make a choice.

- CHECKBOX—Is similar to the radio button. It lets the visitor make a choice using his mouse to click on a box.

- POP-UP BOX—Also known as a drop-down menu lets choose from a menu of items which pop up or drop down.

When creating forms for your site, you can use any of these or a combination of any of these. To use them, you need to know the commands that correspond to each. The following are those commands:

```
Text Box: <INPUT TYPE="text" NAME="name" SIZE="in
characters">
```

INPUT TYPE tells the program that a form item is to be placed here and that the form item is a text box. The "text" tells the program that it's to be a text box.

NAME is the name you want to give this text box. This area is for your benefit. These forms are emailed to you in text form. The NAME tells you what form is being sent to you. What you receive is an email that has name=(the name you gave the box) and then the information your visitor provided in the form. So you want to give this text box a name that's relevant to the text box's purpose. Therefore if you want to use a text box to have the visitors provide you with their email addresses you'd name this box "email."

SIZE tells the program how many characters you want it to be. Just be sure to give enough room for the visitor to type the text you're requesting.

```
Text Area Box: <TEXTAREA NAME="name you want for
the box" ROWS="number of rows you want" COLS="num-
ber of columns you want"></TEXTAREA>
```

The TEXTAREA tells the program that this is another form item and that it will be a text area box. NAME is the same as it is for the text box. ROWS and COLS lets you set how many rows you want in the text area box and how many characters you want for each row.

```
Radio Button: <INPUT TYPE="radio" NAME="heading for
button" VALUE="button name">button name
```

The INPUT TYPE and NAME are the same for the text box command. You indicate the type of form item after the INPUT TYPE and the name you want for this type of form page. The Value lets you give the button a name that shows up to the visitor as a choice. Therefore, you must type this command for each radio button you want in your form.

```
Checkbox: <INPUT TYPE="checkbox" NAME="heading for
checkbox" VALUE="name for checkbox">checkbox name
```

Each of these items are the same as they are for the radio buttons. You, again, need one command for each check box you want to include in your form.

Pop-up Box:
```
<SELECT NAME="name for form" SIZE="size of box in
lines">
<OPTION SELECTED>Option
```

QUICK ☞ PAINLESS

The **TEXTAREA** box command requires the </TEXTAREA> closing tag. The **TEXT** box doesn't.

continues

continued

```
<OPTION>Option
<OPTION>Option
(and so forth for as many selections as you want)
</SELECT>
```

SELECT tells the program that another form is to be placed here and that it's a SELECT or pop-up form. NAME is the same as for the other form items. SIZE tells the program the size you want for the box in lines. Generally one line is sufficient. OPTION SELECTED tells the program which item in your menu list will appear in the box. OPTION tells the program what other items you want in the menu list. /SELECT closes the command.

To finish off your form you need to include a way for the visitors to submit the form to you. Generally you need a Submit and Reset button. The Reset button lets them clear the form and start over if they think they've made a mistake in filling it out. Following is the command for these two buttons:

```
<INPUT TYPE="submit"><INPUT TYPE="reset>
```

When you want to use a variety of these form items in your form, you have to let the program know to separate them. Inserting a line break <BR> and/or a paragraph tag <P> accomplishes this for you. You place a line break command for each addition line you want to appear between form times. You also need to type the name for the form item or instructions to the visitor before or after the command in order for it to show up on the page.

So if we wanted to create a form to ask our visitors to give us a little information about their pets, and we

YOU'LL THANK YOURSELF LATER

You must place your email address directly after the "mailto:" tag. Be sure there is no space between the tag and your address.

wanted to include all of these form items, it might look like this:

```
<FORM METHOD="POST" ACTION="mailto:me@isp.com">
<INPUT TYPE="text" NAME="Pet's name" SIZE="30">Pet's
Name<BR>
<BR>
```

Other pets and their names<TEXTAREA NAME="Other pets and their names" ROWS=6 COLS=50></TEXTAREA>

```
<BR>
<P>Type of Pet
<P><INPUT TYPE="radio" NAME="Type of Pet"
VALUE="cat">cat<BR>
<P><INPUT TYPE="radio" NAME="Type of Pet"
VALUE="dog">dog<BR>
<P><INPUT TYPE="radio" NAME="Type of Pet"
VALUE="bird">bird<BR>
<P><INPUT TYPE="radio" NAME="Type of Pet"
VALUE="fish">fish<BR>
```

Living arrangements

```
<P><INPUT TYPE="checkbox" NAME="Living arrangements"
VALUE="indoors">Indoors<BR>
<P><INPUT TYPE="checkbox" NAME="Living arrangements"
VALUE="outdoors">Outdoors<BR>
<P><INPUT TYPE="checkbox" NAME="Living arrangements"
VALUE="cage">Cage<BR>
<P><INPUT TYPE="checkbox" NAME="Living arrangements"
VALUE="bowl">Bowl<BR>
<BR>
<P>Choice for next pet
<P><SELECT NAME="Choice for next pet" SIZE="1">
<OPTION SELECTED>cat
<OPTION>dog
<OPTION>bird
<OPTION>fish
</SELECT><BR>
<P><INPUT TYPE="submit"><INPUT TYPE="reset">
</FORM>
```

Whew! That was a lot of work. This gives you a form with all the form items in it. See Figure 11.2 for an example of how this code makes the page look with the form inserted.

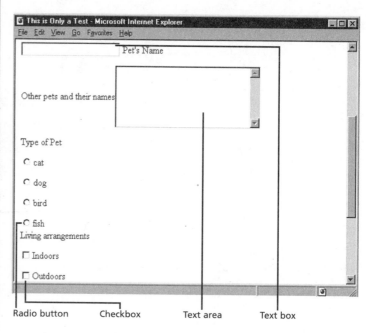

Radio button   Checkbox   Text area   Text box

Figure 11.2   *Browser view of a form created manually.*

Let Your Web Page Editor Do It for You

I don't know about you, but that's a bit too much typing for me and way too much work. I think I'll let my Web editor do it for me.

In the editor you choose to use, select the FORM icon or command. Some editors give you a dialog box and require you to enter information for each of the items, while others have different commands you select and enter the text in the appropriate areas.

For instance, the HTML Notes editor gives you a dialog box that helps you create a form. See Figure 11.3 for an example of this dialog box.

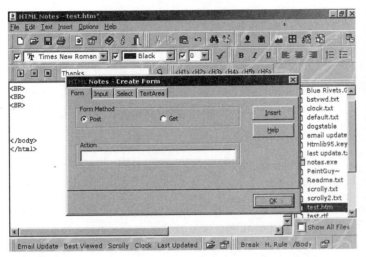

Figure 11.3 *Create Form dialog box for the HTML Notes HTML editor.*

With the Arachnophilia editor, you select the form item type you want to insert by selecting Commands, Form. Then you fill in the areas to customize the form to your needs.

Both programs enter the code for you. All you need to do is enter how you want the form items presented and the custom information you want in your form.

That's much easier than typing in all those codes yourself, don't you think? And there's less chance of you making a mistake. If you want more information on how to do create forms, there are several sites on the Web that can help you. Two of these sites are ZDnet's Garage at `www.zdnet.com/products/garage/`, or at CNet's Builder.com at `www.builder.com`.

Congratulations! You've tackled a major hurdle in building your site. Forms are the most tedious and sometimes the most difficult element to master. You deserve to treat yourself to something special. Schedule yourself a day at the spa or a day of golf. Relax and know that if you can do forms, you can do anything!

The Lazy Way

I'VE BEEN FRAMED

Frames are subwindows or cells within a page. They're used to separate different categories of information.

Frames give you a way to display multiple Web pages on one browser screen. The code lets you split the browser screen into multiple parts.

They can be a little bit overwhelming at first. But once you learn the basics, you'll master them in no time.

What you're doing with frames is a little different than anything else you've done in your pages. In essence you're creating a template where more than one page can sit. Here is the basic command to create a frames page template:

```
<HTML>
<TITLE>First Frame Page Title</TITLE>
<FRAMESET COL="percent of page for columns">
<FRAME SRC="first page address">
<FRAME SRC="second page address">
(and so on for each frame page)
</FRAMESET>
</HTML>
```

FRAMESET starts the frame page. It tells the browser a visitor is using the frames that are placed here.

COLS tells the program that you want columns in your frame. You can indicate how many columns and the percentage you want them to occupy on the page. For multiple columns, separate the percentages by commas. The total percentages for all the columns must add up to 99% or 100%.

QUICK ● PAINLESS

Create the pages you want to use in your frames first. This enables you to see how they'll look when you do create the frame page template. It also gives you the address for the pages that you need when creating the frames page.

FRAME SRC gives the program the source of the frame or the address for the frame. The /FRAMESET tag ends the command.

In addition to columns, you can add rows to your frames. The command is <FRAMESET ROWS="percentage of page rows are to occupy">. You add this command after the FRAMESET COLS command. Just like for COLS, you can have as many rows as you want as long as the percentages add up to 99% or 100%. You add this command each time for each frameset you have in your pages. Just remember to end each frameset before you begin a new one.

Each address must be for a page you have on your Web site. They can also be other people's pages. For these frames to work you need to create the pages and have an address for them. We'll talk more about getting addresses for the pages in your site in Chapter 12.

Therefore, if you wanted to create a page with two framesets and two rows in each frameset, here is how the command would look:

```
<HTML>
<TITLE>FIRST FRAMESET</TITLE>
<FRAMESET ROWS="50%,50%>
<FRAME SRC="1stpage address">
<FRAME SRC="2ndpage address">
</FRAMESET>
```

Let's take a look at this. See Figure 11.4 for an example of how this frame looks in a page.

QUICK PAINLESS

You don't have to make the pages you want displayed in your frame's template the size of the columns or rows in it. The browser makes the page fit the frame.

Frames

Figure 11.4 *Browser view of frames in a page.*

Now that wasn't so hard. Frames look much more intimidating than they actually are.

What about the visitors that aren't able to view frames or don't want to? You can offer an option to let those viewers of your site see it without the frames. There are two ways you can handle this. One is write a second page without frames and offer the visitor a choice between the two. The other option is to use the <NOFRAME></NOFRAME> command. Here is how this NOFRAME command looks:

```
<FRAMESET COLS="50%,50%>
<NOFRAME>
```

Enter a message to visitors explaining how to get to a non-frame version of your pages.

```
</NOFRAME>
```

(the rest of your frameset commands)

In real time, this is how this command might look:

```
<FRAMESET COLS="50%,50%">
<NOFRAME>
```

Hello Web surfer. This page is set up to offer frames. If you're reading this message, you either don't have the capabilities to view pages with frames or choose not to. I try to please all my visitors. Please go to <A HREF:"http://(non-frame page address)">this page</A> for a non-frame version of this page.

```
</NOFRAME>
(the rest of the frames commands)
</FRAMESET>
</HTML>
```

These commands will get you started in creating frame pages. But there's got to be an easier way.

Let Your Web Page Editor Do It for You

Most of the HTML editors have a Frame Wizard or Frame commands. Of course the ones that have Frame Wizards are easier to work with. But the ones with commands or icons are almost as easy. They just take a few more steps to complete.

Whichever option your editor offers, either follow the steps in the Wizard or the steps outlined in the previous section.

For instance, the Site Builder editor has a Frames Wizard. Therefore when we use that editor, we click on the Frames Icon that looks like a page broken into four different colored frames. Site Builder then gives you a dialog box that asks you if you want to use columns or

rows and how many frames you want. See Figure 11.5 for an example of this dialog box.

Figure 11.5   *Frames Wizard dialog box in the Site*

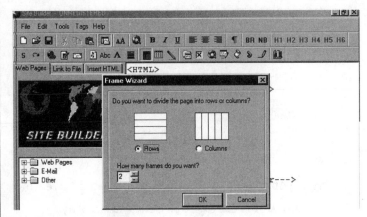

Builder Web editor.

When you select the number of frames you want and select whether you want rows or columns, click the OK button. Then you get another dialog box that has numerous frames (1 through 8) to let you indicate the page address for each frame and how you want the scroll bar to appear—Auto, Yes, or No.

You simply type in the address of each page you want to appear in each frame. When you're done, click the OK button to enter the frames codes into your edit page. That's all there is to it. Your page is now set up for frames. That was almost too easy.

If you would like more information on how to create frames in your pages, go to the ZDnet Garage site or the

Builder.com site mentioned previously. Both have excellent information on various elements like these and others you can add to your site.

Just in case you need some more encouragement, see Figure 11.6 for an example of a page viewed in a browser and Figure 11.7 for an example of what the source code looks like in the Arachnophilia editor.

Figure 11.6 *Browser view of a page with frames.*

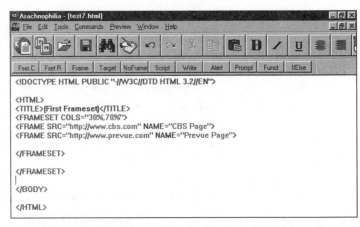

```
Arachnophilia - [test7.html]
File  Edit  Tools  Commands  Preview  Window  Help

Fset C  Fset R  Frame  Target  NoFrame  Script  Write  Alert  Prompt  Funct  IfElse

<!DOCTYPE HTML PUBLIC "-//W3C//DTD HTML 3.2//EN">

<HTML>
<TITLE>First Frameset</TITLE>
<FRAMESET COLS="30%,70%">
<FRAME SRC="http://www.cbs.com" NAME="CBS Page">
<FRAME SRC="http://www.prevue.com" NAME="Prevue Page">

</FRAMESET>

</FRAMESET>

</BODY>

</HTML>
```

Figure 11.7   *Edit page in the Arachnophilia HTML editor showing the source code for Frames.*

HEAR ME ROAR

Audio adds enhancement to your site much the same way that soundtracks add to the whole movie experience. They are fairly easy to include in your pages. But be aware that they require your visitors to have sound capabilities or extra utilities in order to hear them.

Most computers manufactured within the past three years are equipped with built-in audio capabilities. These audio capabilities enable visitors to list to WAV files, which are a form of sound files. You can also record your own sound files provided you have a microphone.

Audio files come in several varieties—wav, .midi, .aiff, and .au files. There are two ways you can get audio files for your pages. One way is to make your own and the other is to download them from an online audio library.

IF YOU'RE SO
INCLINED

You can find audio files at these sites:

Pete's TV WAVs—
www.tvwavs.com/

Yahoo!'s WAV collection—
www.yahoo.com/Computers_
and_Internet/Multimedia/
Sound/Archives/WAV/

The Sound Ring—
www.nidlink.com/~ruger/
ring.html

The MIDI Farm—
www.midifarm.com/files/
midifilies/General_MIDI/

Once you have an audio file you want to use, it's easy to add it to your page. You use the link command with the address of the sound file. The command would look like this:

```
<A HREF="sound file address">Name of sound</A>.
```

Or you can enter a command that automatically starts playing a sound when the page loads. The command looks like this:

```
<BGSOUND SRC="sound file" LOOP=1>
```

It's that easy! Of course your editor makes it even more simple. When you use your HTML editor, simply click on the Insert Sound icon, if it has one and fill in the boxes in the dialog box that appears. You'll need to select the sound file you want to use from your hard drive. That means if you want to use a file from a sound archive off the Web, you'll have to save that file to your hard drive.

CAUGHT ON TAPE

Video is an excellent element you can add to your site to give it more pizzazz. However, in order for you audience to experience it, they have to have the utilities to enable them to view video. Video requires an extra program such as Real Audio for visitors to fully experience your site. Fortunately Real Audio is freeware and they welcome links to their site to allow people to download it. Real Audio lets you hear sounds as well as view video. Other types of video can be viewed via plug-ins or other utilities.

Videos and/or movies come in two formats; MPEG, which stands for Motion Picture Experts Group, and Quick Time. MPEG is pretty much the standard format used in Web pages. It tends to be more universal than Quick Time.

Be aware that when you move into using video, you're getting into disk space issues. Video files are generally much larger than image files. They can present manageability problems.

The command to insert video into your pages is the link command, just like it is for audio. The command would look like this:

```
<A HREF="video file address">name of file</A>
```

This command causes the file to open in another new window. Most video you come across on the Web does play in a separate window. It can pop up in a video player window, or on a new page.

Most of the Web editors don't have a quick function for adding video to your pages. Therefore you'll have to add it yourself manually. But since it's only a hyperlink code with the address for the video file in it, that shouldn't be a problem. You can click on the Link icon and type in the address of the video file and give the link a name, if you prefer.

In addition to requiring your visitors to acquire additional utilities in order to view your presentations, you need special equipment to present videos. You either need a video cam or a digital video cam. If you use a regular video cam, then you have to have the video converted to digital format. Digital video cams are rather pricey at the moment. And the quality is rather poor.

Therefore, instead of taking you through the steps of a project, we'll just show you the code in a page with video, the page linking to the video, and the video. See Figure 11.8 for an example of the video.

Figure 11.8 *WFAA News broadcast using live video on their page.*

CHATTING IT UP

Offering chat as part of your site is something you might consider. However, you might not want to consider it for long. It requires a lot of time and effort on your part. It also requires your visitor, in many cases, to install an additional utility in order to chat.

Providing chat for your users also requires you to provide some complicated scripting to program it into your page. Scripting is beyond the scope of this book. However, you can find references about where to learn scripting in the "If You Really Want More, Read These" section at the end of this book.

Just to give you an idea of how chat is offered on the Web, in case you haven't already run across a chat room or two, we'll show you how a site handles chat and how the chat appears. See Figure 11.9 for an example of chat rooms offered and Figure 11.10 for an example of a Web chat.

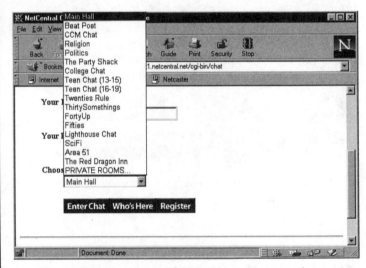

Figure 11.9 *NetCentral Chat Registration page showing list of chat rooms available.*

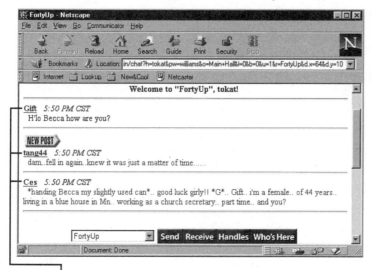

Chat dialog between users

Figure 11.10 *NetCentral FortyUp chat room.*

Generally, in Web chat rooms, you have to refresh or reload the page every few seconds to see any new conversation. This makes it hard to keep up with the chat.

There are some chat utilities that let you connect directly to IRC (Internet Relay Chat), a real-time chat service of the Internet, but they can difficult to set up in your page.

In this chapter you learned about some of the more advanced HTML you might want to use to enhance the look of your pages. Some of these advanced features included marquees, animation, forms, frames, background sounds, video, and timestamps. You're a Web Master extraordinaire now! Your site is ready to post to the Web. Let's rush to the next chapter and learn how to hang our pages.

Part 4

Final Cut

twelve

Hide and Seek

You have taken great care and spent your time designing and building your special Web site. You planned it so that it would give the proper information to your visitors and convey the right meaning about your company. You have created a masterpiece. Now what do you do with it? It's absolutely no good to you sitting on your hard drive.

Your purpose in building your Web site is so that you can get it on the Web for the thousands, or millions, of people around the world to see. This chapter is going to show you how to get your Web site on the Web.

I WANT TO BE PUBLISHED

Haven't you always wanted to be published? Well, now's your chance. It's not quite the same as seeing your name or byline on a book, in a magazine, or in a newspaper, but it's publishing all the same.

Now that you have spent all this time and care in creating your Web presence, or pages, and you have completed your goal, it's time to get those pages onto the Web for the world

to see. In Internet jargon, putting your Web presence on the WWW is called *hanging* your pages.

The first thing you need to do is contact your provider to find out how much Web space you have and what address you need to use. Generally the ISP gives you an address that starts with its *domain address*, such as `http://www.isp.com`. A domain address is an address name which a person or business registers as its own. For instance, cbs.com, swbell.com, and so forth.

Then the ISP gives you the extension for your address. Usually this addition is your sign on or ID. For instance, my address is `http://www.flash.net/~tokat`. The www.flash.net is my provider's domain name address and the ~tokat is my home page or site address. It is also my sign on with the ISP.

After you have your address you can start uploading your pages to that address. You'll be doing this via File Transfer Protocol (FTP). FTP is software and a service of the Internet that enables you to transfer your Web page files from your computer to the Web server.

You have to upload your files onto your ISP's FTP site in the correct directory. Once you do that, your pages appear on the Web. So, while you have your ISP on the phone, ask them on what directory you'll need to load your pages. You also need to find out how to log onto their FTP site. Some providers give you this information on their own Web pages, but if they don't, a few questions to technical service people get you the information you need.

Here are the questions you need to ask:

1. The address to the ISP's FTP site.

2. The log-in ID to use (usually your sign on name).

3. The password you need to use (usually your sign on password).

4. Into what directory and folder to upload your files. Be sure to have the ISP give you the address it has assigned to you for Web pages.

5. How much space you have on the Web server.

Some providers charge a one-time set up fee when you want to hang pages on their service. Some providers charge businesses with a larger fee than they do individuals and some even charge a monthly fee for businesses that want to hang their pages on their system. Be sure to find out what your provider charges in this respect. If you're not happy with what your provider is going to charge you, shop around on the Web, there are many services that will hang your pages for a fee or let you hang your pages on their server for a fee.

After you have all this information, you will need to log onto your provider and access FTP through an FTP *client*. Client is Internet lingo for software.

After you have an FTP client downloaded and installed, launch it. Once it's running, you'll need the information you received from your ISP—remember those questions you asked? Here's where the answers come in handy. Next, follow these steps:

YOU'LL THANK YOURSELF LATER

If you don't have an FTP client, you can find several good ones on the Web. One site that has some excellent Internet software is the Tucows site at www.tucows.com. WS_FTP is probably one of the best FTP clients available, but there are others you can choose from at that site. FTP software is extremely useful and good to have.

1. Enter the address of the computer to which you want to connect.

   This is the ISP's computer. It's also called a Host. It's the remote computer that hosts your pages, or holds them.

2. Next, enter your user ID, or sign on, and your password in the boxes provided.

3. Click the button to connect to the FTP site.

   See Figure 12.1 for an example of the sign on screen for FTP.

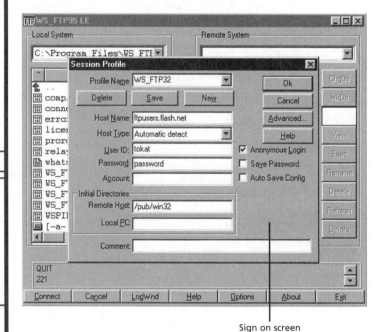

Sign on screen

Figure 12.1. *WS_FTP log on screen.*

You're now on the FTP site for your provider. Notice your screen is split into two sections. On the left side is the local section and on the right is the remote section. The local section is you. It holds a directory of all the files on your computer. The remote side is your provider. You need to make sure you're in the directory to upload your pages to your provider's Web server.

Now transfer your Web site files from your computer to the directory of the provider's computer. Here are the steps you follow:

4. First find the directory that houses your Web site files. You'll find it on the local side under the folder for the Web editor you used to create them.

5. Highlight all the files you want to transfer from your computer to the provider's. This includes all the .htm or .html files that are your pages as well as all the graphics, audio, and video files you included in those pages.

6. Click on the right pointing arrow to start the transfer process. This tells the program to copy the files from your computer over to the remote computer.

7. Sit back and watch as your files transfer, or go fix yourself a cup of coffee. This will take a few minutes, depending on the size of the files you're transferring and/or the number of files. See Figure 12.2 for an example of the transfer window.

YOU'LL THANK YOURSELF LATER

Your home page must be named an index file for most providers. Therefore, if your home page doesn't have the address of index.htm or index.html, then you need to rename it so that it does. Otherwise you'll get a page that has none of the things you designed on it. It will only display an index directory of the files in your site.

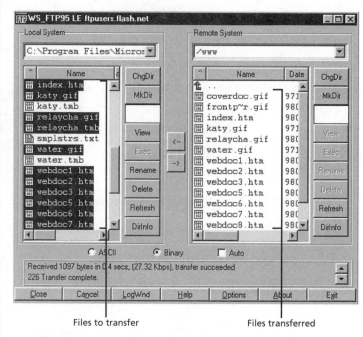

Files to transfer   Files transferred

Figure 12.2 *WS_FTP transfer window showing files highlighted and transferred.*

After you have uploaded all the files relevant to your Web pages, go to your address (URL) and make sure your pages look the way you designed them. If they aren't correct, go back to FTP and remove them. Then you need to find out why they aren't presenting on the Web as you designed them. Sometimes this might mean extensions to your files aren't compatible with the Web, sometimes it could be a simple fix in your design codes. If you have problems that you can't find the solution to on your own, call your technical service line for your provider. They should be able and willing to help you fix any problems.

LET THE SEARCH BEGIN

All the learning, planning, and designing you've done to build your site is an accomplishment you should be proud of. But the really fun part comes when people come to visit your site. Before you can have visitors, they have to find you.

After you have your site built it's time to list or register it with the various search engines. You want to register your site with as many of the search engines as you can, especially the major engines such as Yahoo!, Altavista, Excite, Lycos, and so forth.

You can register with any or all of these sites yourself. However, that can be quite time consuming. Using this method you have to contact each search engine and request to be added. This usually involves filling out a form for each engine separately. There are hundreds of search engines, so you can see this might take days.

I sure don't have that kind of time and I know you don't either. Well, there's a much faster and easier way. There are Web site registering services that do all the work for you. With these services you'll fill out one form which they use to register your site on many search engines.

Some of these site registering services register your site with a certain number of engines at no charge and offer an additional package to register with more engines for a fee. These services register your site for you quickly, so the investment is often worth it. That's a decision for you to make.

QUICK **⬛** PAINLESS

Prepare a dynamic sentence or two describing your site ahead of time. Many search engines ask for this as part of their submission process.

QUICK **⬛** PAINLESS

If you choose to register your site yourself, here's a site that lists many search engines and lets you submit your registration from its site: OB Home Net— obnet.com/services/search_submit.html.

In addition to these site registration services, you can also use another service to see if your site is registered with those search engines. One site that does this for you at no charge is called Did-it.com. Its address is www.did-it.com. It's a quick way to verify that you are listed with the search engines you want to be listed with. However, give these engines time to get you registered. It sometimes takes a week or two (or more) for them to process your site's information.

By far this is the ideal route to take. If you think you might have the time, there is one more option. You can download software that allows you to register with numerous search engines at one time. This software is called site promotion software.

With these types of programs you fill in a simple form which the program uses to batch-process the submissions. These programs can save you time and work. They operate quickly and give you progress feedback. When the job is done you can check your ranking with the built-in utility. This utility checks your site with the search engines and tells you how you rank with them.

One of these three methods will help you get your site registered with the various search engines. You decide which one works better for you and your schedule.

AND NOW ANNOUNCING...

There are several ways you can announce your site to the world. One way is to mass mail or email everyone you know. This is an excellent way to get the word out.

Another way is to make sure all your stationery, business cards, and any print or advertising you may do has your Web site address included as part of your address. This lets everyone who receives correspondence from you or who you give your cards to know that you are on the Web and where to find you.

And lastly, you can register with the What's New or Web indexes. These are the What's New, What's Cool, online directories, and other announcement-type sites.

Following are some of these sites, their categories, and addresses:

What's New Pages:

- Special Connections—`sirius.we.lc.ehu.es/internet/inet.services.html`

- Netscape's What's New Page—`home.netscape.com/netcenter/new.html`

Web Indexes:

- The World Wide Web Virtual Library—`vlib.org/Overview.html`

- The Living City—`www.cadvision.com/top.html`

Business Only Sites:

- Open Market—`www.directory.net/`

- Biz Web—`www.bizweb.com/`

- Product.com —`www.product.com/`

There are probably dozens more sites just like these. A search would give you a better list, but this should get you started.

Then, of course, there are fee-based advertisement sites. These sites charge a fee and require you to join their organizations. For that fee, you get a listing with them and a link from their page to yours.

In addition to these sites, there is a mailing list that announces new Web sites. It's called Net-Happenings. You can subscribe to this list by sending an email to `majordomo@is.internic.net` with "subscribe net-happenings" in the body of the message. To submit an announcement of your site to this list of thousands of subscribers, send it to net-happenings@is.internic.net after you have subscribed to the list. After you make your announcement, you might want to unsubscribe from this list. It's a huge list and you'll start receiving bucketloads of mail from it. To unsubscribe, follow the directions in the introductory document you will receive from the list.

You are now armed with everything you need to know to get your site posted to the Web. After your site is up, you can register it with all the different search engines and know that people from around the world will soon be visiting it. To make sure everyone you know is aware that you now have a Web site, use print media to let them know, and to announce your site.

All the effort you've put into building your site and hanging it on the Web has accomplished most of your goals. But how are you to know if your site is really working with your visitors? You don't—unless you give them a way to let you know their thoughts. Chapter 13 shows you how to get feedback from your visitors and how to let them contact you.

Wave to the Audience

Now that you have your killer site designed and you're ready to hang it on the Web, there's one more thing to consider. How are your visitors going to contact you? How can they tell you what they like or don't like? How can you get feedback from them?

No matter how hard we work or how hard we try to prevent them, things go wrong. Because you can't monitor your site 24 hours a day, you need a way for your visitors to contact you if a problem arises.

Providing contact information also gives your visitors the chance to give you positive feedback. Praise is always pleasant to hear.

There are a couple of ways you can let visitors contact you and give you the feedback you want. One is by including contact information and the other is through a guestbook.

IT'S IN THE MAIL

One complaint that's heard most often about Web sites is that there is no contact information for the visitor to let the owner or designer know of problems or to ask questions. I know, you

say, but if I place my email address in my site, I'll start getting mass mail from advertisers.

This is true. You likely will, especially when you register with the search engines. But that's a necessary evil you'll have to put up with so that you can be there for your visitors when they need you. So just place your email address in your site, preferably on several pages if you have a big site. It's easy to delete unwanted email—much easier than losing visitors.

Placing your email address on your pages is easy. It's just a link with your email address as the link. The command is

```
<A HREF="mailto:your email address">keyword</A>
```

Most of the HTML editors have an icon you can click to insert an email link. Click on the icon and type in the address and the description for the link.

If someone else designs your site, you might want to include his or her email address also. Many sites list this as the Webmaster's address. The code would look like this:

```
<A HREF="mailto:webmaster@isp.com">Webmaster</A>
```

If this is a business site, you might also want to consider including the email address of the customer service department, technical assistance department, key officers or management for the business, and so forth. The easier you make it for the customer to contact your people, the better service you are offering them. Even if they are complaining, they remember the service they get all along the way. When it's hard for them to get the information they need it only makes them madder and harder to deal with. Including this information in your site is easy and provides so much for your visitors.

SIGN HERE, PLEASE

Another great way to provide a service to your visitors is to include a *guestbook* in your site. The guestbook lets them indicate that they visited your site and tell you what they thought or ask any questions.

There are three different types of guestbooks you can offer on your site. One is the simple "mailto:" guestbook, another is a guestbook that offers a page thanking the visitor for writing, and the last is a guestbook that posts what your visitors write to a separate page.

The guestbook with a page thanking the visitor for writing and the guestbook that posts what the visitors write to a separate page require CGI scripting, which is beyond the scope of this book. Therefore, they won't be covered in any detail here.

Guestbooks not only let the visitor tell you what they think about your site, but they also let you gather information about your visitors. You can ask visitors to give you their name, email address, Web site address, age, and so forth. For business, this information can come in handy for market research reports or other marketing activities. For the individual, it can give you an idea of the type of visitors you have coming to your site. So a guestbook can benefit not only the visitor, but you also can use the information you get from your guestbook to email periodic updates to let your visitors know what's new on your page.

QUICK ⊕ PAINLESS

The "mailto:" tells the Web server to open the visitor's email program to send an email to the address provided after the "mailto:".

Be sure to check this guestbook in several browsers. The mailto: code doesn't work the same in some of the older browsers. It only opens the email program but doesn't address the email to the mailto: address.

A guestbook is a form altered to include the information you want for your book. See Figure 13.1 for an example of a guestbook included in a site.

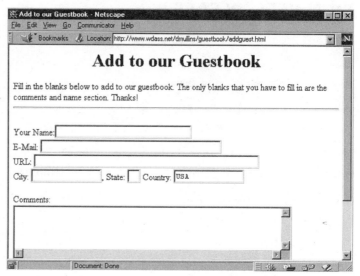

Figure 13.1   *Guestbook in Debra Mullins site.*

If you wanted to create a simple "mailto:" guest book, the code might look like this:

```
<H1>Sign in Please . . .</H1>
<FORM METHOD="POST" ACTION="mailto:user@isp.com">
<B>Please enter your name: </B><INPUT NAME="user-
name" SIZE="30"><BR>
<B>and your email address</B><INPUT NAME="usermail"
SIZE="30">
<B>and your home page address</B><INPUT
NAME="userurl" SIZE="150">
<P>
<CENTER>
<B>What do you think of my site</B>
<P>
<INPUT TYPE="radio" NAME="I_think_that
VALUE="It's_great"> It's Great!
<INPUT TYPE="radio" NAME="I_think_that
VALUE="It's_horrible">It's horrible!
```

```
<INPUT TYPE="radio" NAME="do_better
VALUE="My_dog_could_do_better"> My dog could do bet-
ter!
<INPUT TYPE-"radio" NAME="quit_job"
VALUE="Don't_quit">Don't quit your day job!
<P>
</CENTER>
<H3>Use the space below to make any additional com-
ments</H3>
<CENTER>
<TEXTAREA NAME="comment" ROWS=6 COLS=60></TEXTAREA>
<P>
<B>Thank you for your input</B>
<BR>
<INPUT TYPE="submit" VALUE="Send it!">
<INPUT TYPE="reset" VALUE="Start over">
</CENTER>
</FORM>
```

See Figure 13.2 for an example of how this code looks when viewed in a browser.

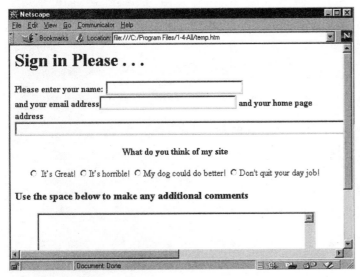

Figure 13.2 *Browser view of a guestbook.*

With this guestbook code, you begin with a header to tell the visitor what you want them to do. Then you

 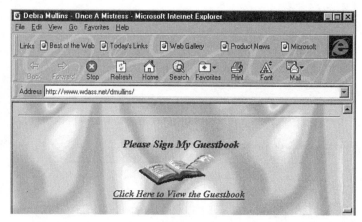
begin the form and tell the Web server what kind of form it's to be—POST. For the ACTION you tell the server you want the results mailed to you and provide your mailto: address. Then you follow the normal form format adding text between each form item.

It's fairly easy to create. Of course if you use your HTML editor it's much simpler than typing all the codes yourself. Just click on the Forms icon and insert the values where needed. If you need a refresher, refer to Chapter 11 and the section about forms. All you've done to set up this guestbook is use two textboxes, a few radio buttons, and a text box.

This guestbook would be on a page all by itself. Therefore, you need a link to that page. See Figure 13.3 for an example of the link to the guestbook in Figure 13.1.

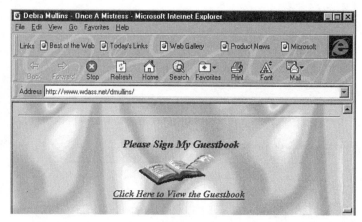

Figure 13.3 *Debra Mullin's site showing a guestbook link.*

If you'd like to use a similar guestbook link, you'd have to get the guestbook image from one of the clip art or graphics sites, and use a font color that's compatible with your site.

That's all there is to it. You now have a link to your guestbook and a guestbook. All you have to do is sit back and wait for your visitors to start signing in and giving you their comments.

Visitors need a way to contact you. Including contact information for yourself, your Web designer, or for key personnel in your company is one way to give your visitors what they want. The other way is to let them express their feelings about your site through a guestbook. The guestbook provides a service to them while it lets you collect important information about them.

Now that you have your site ready and up on the Web, it's time to learn how to boost the number of visitors you can attract. Chapter 14 shows you just how to go about this.

QUICK PAINLESS

If the data doesn't arrive to you in an email as text, it can come as an attachment. The attachment has the .dat extension, which stands for data. You can read this file by opening it in a text editor such as Note Pad or by changing the extension to .txt for text.

Chapter fourteen

Open the Floodgates

All your hard work and planning has finally paid off. You've built an awesome site! It's up on the Web, ready to be viewed. But the only people who have seen it so far are your friends and your mother. Exciting—about as exciting as watching paint dry.

You want excitement. You want people everywhere to see your masterpiece. The more people, the better!

If you've created a business site, the number of people who visit your site is extremely important. The more people who see your site, the more chances you have of selling your products or services.

When people come to your site, this is called *hits*. The more hits you get, the better able you are to generate revenue. One form of revenue you can get by increasing your hits is through advertising. If you've surfed the Web at all, you've undoubtedly seen all the banner ads on the various sites. They're there because those sites are good sources for the ads and/or because they get a large number of hits.

Then as you boost your hits, you also need to know how effective your site is for your visitors. You want to know where

TRY MISSPELLING FOR A CHANGE

One way to make sure your site appears more often in search engines is to misspell your keywords and provide several variations. Often visitors misspell the search terms they're looking for. Think of ways keywords can be misspelled or mistyped and include those in your META tags.

they go, where they linger, and what interests them about your pages.

PUMP ME UP

Your first step in boosting your hits is to register your site with the search engines. You learned how to do this in Chapter 12. Review that chapter if you need a refresher.

Search engines are the number one tool people use to find your site. The higher your ranking with those search engines, the more you increase your chances of getting seen.

Meta tags, covered in Chapter 11, are the way search engines catalog sites. The search sites use *robots* or "bots" to catalog sites. Robots, also called spiders, crawl the Web looking for specific information. They are automated programs designed to perform specific activities like searching the Web for keywords or email addresses. These robots use the first clumps of data they recognize as text to determine the description for your site.

When people search for Web pages using these search engines, they are searching by keywords that describe the information they want. These robots do the same thing in essence. They rank sites or pages by how many times a keyword appears in the document.

You can increase your ranking with these search engines by using META tags to tell these robots about your site. If you do it wrong, you decrease your chances of getting visitors or showing up on these search engines.

The recommendation is that these tags should not exceed 1,000 characters in length. Therefore, think carefully about the keywords you want to use in these META tags. Keep your list of keywords short and relevant to topics your site covers.

Search engines are cracking down on abuse of the META tag method of increasing a site's rating with them. Following are some things you should avoid doing:

- *Word Stuffing.* Cramming META tags full of keywords that don't relate to your site in order to match a search return more often.

- *Metajacking.* Stealing the META tags from another site that gets high rankings with search engines and using it in your site.

- *Spamdexing.* Using the same keyword over and over in your comments tags.

- *Fontmatching.* Adding keywords to your page with the text set for the same color as the background so the type is invisible, but still is indexed with the search engines.

To increase the hits to your site, you need to put a little effort into promoting your site. There are some wonderful site promotion tools you can use. TagGen is a tool that creates META tags for you. WebPosition is a tool that tells you how your site ranks with the search engines and tells you ways you can increase your rankings. You can find these at the ZDnet products site—`hotfiles.zdnet.com/cgi-bin/texis/swlib/hotfiles/`. Then do a search for either site promotion tools or for these specific programs. Combining proper use of META tags and site promotion tools can help you increase the number of hits you get on your site.

HOW DO I RATE?

After you have your site up and registered with the search engines, you'll start getting visitors. These visitors will be people who are interested in what your site is about.

You may or may not be interested in knowing who your audience is. But maybe you should be. Knowing who your audience is helps you keep your site interesting to the people who visit it.

There are many things visitors can tell you about themselves and about your site. They can tell you what they like about your site. You can also learn how they get to your site and where they go while there. And if you handle it right, you can also get vital statistics about them, such as their gender, age, income group, and so forth.

All these bits of information are helpful in updating and designing your site so that it's more beneficial to your visitors. You can gather and analyze all this information yourself by using specially designed tools, or you can let someone else do it for you.

Tracking and analyzing the traffic to your site can help you generate more traffic. Knowing what really interests your visitors helps you deliver more of what they want, which keeps people coming back to your site.

Before you can analyze your site's traffic you need a basic understanding about how it works. There are basi-

YOU'LL THANK YOURSELF LATER

You need to know the importance of profiling the visitors to your site. Once you know what's important, you can select the program or service that will work best for your traffic analysis needs.

cally two ways to analyze your traffic. One is to get copies of the log files for your site. Most Web servers generate these.

These files include information such as the visitors' IP (Internet Provider) addresses, the date and time they visited, the files they accessed, where they came from, and the type of browser they used. These log files require no special tools—just your time.

The other way to analyze your site traffic is to use analysis tools to track each visitor and their activities while they are at your site. These tools give you a more accurate reading about what interests your visitors.

There are several good log file analysis tools available. Some of these include Aquas's Bazaar Analyzer and WebTrends. Both of these and others can be found at the ZDnet site at `hotfiles.zdnet.com/cgi-bin/texis/swlib/` `hotfiles/`. A search for log file analyzers or Web traffic tools will give you a good list of software to choose from.

To get more specific information about your visitors requires that you ask them for that information. This is where the forms covered in Chapter 11 come in handy. Gathering this information and combining it with the log file information lets you develop, expand, and refine the content you offer. If this information tells you that your audience is very different than you thought it was going to be, you can adjust your site's content, product line, and features to capture the audience you originally wanted or to keep the audience you've attracted.

In addition, you can also count the hits to each of your pages or files. This lets you know which pages your

YOU'LL THANK YOURSELF LATER

Some analysis tools track visitors by assuming each user with the same IP address and same browser is a unique visitor. They look at the log files line by line and count up the matches. Tying technical transaction data to actual people isn't all that reliable. So, before you choose an analysis tool, learn how it tracks visitors.

visitors are most interested in and also gives you a higher hit count. Web space providers can give you a hit count broken down by page.

When choosing a Web traffic analysis tool, here's what you should consider:

- *Real-time report access.* Ability to get data concerning the last ten minutes of your site's activity and view it in several graphical formats.

- *Data drill-down.* Gives you different dimensions and layers of your data, various units of time (such as yearly, quarterly, monthly, weekly, daily, and hourly), and combines different types of data and query the database for what you need.

- *Scalability.* Lets you analyze traffic no matter how large or how many sites you have.

- *Ease of Use.* Easy to use without sacrificing access to information.

If you'd rather not spend your time analyzing all this information yourself, you can let someone else do it for you. There are several third-party auditors that make it their business to analyze Web traffic. Most of these type services charge a fee based on the services they provide. Following are some of these services:

- Audit Bureau of Circulations (ABC) Audit Bureau of Verification Services (ABVS) at www.accessabvs.com

- BPA International at www.bpai.com/

- I/PRO NetLine and I/Audit at www.ipro.com

- Media Metrix at www.mediametrix.com/

- MBInteractive at www.mbinteractive.com/

- RelevantKnowledge at www.relevantknowledge.com/

You are now armed with enough information to increase the hits to your site. In addition, you can analyze your site's traffic and use that information to build a bigger and better site. Or just a better site. Now it's time to learn how to manage your site.

Chapter
fifteen

Stretch Your Muscles

Visitors will keep returning to your site only if it changes regularly, if it doesn't remain the same day after day, week after week, or month after month. The Internet community is a fickle group of people. When sites remain the same, they become bored and follow paths to other pages and could well follow a path into the arms of your competitors.

Naturally, if you offer products on your site, your pages are going to change as you add new or more products to your line. However, these shouldn't be the only changes you make. Your pages should change on a regular basis to keep the attention of Web surfers. For example, take a look at the CBS www.cbs.com, Coca-Cola www.cocacola.com, and MCI www.mci.com sites. Then go back to those sites the next day, in a week, and in a month. Notice that they change the look of their sites often. They do this so that they can keep visitors coming back to them.

A Web presence is an ongoing project. It entails checking on that site as often as possible. Links fail or change or just break as do images. You need to monitor your pages for problems. Then you also want to keep your pages alive by changing their design at least as often as once a month, or more often depending on the content of your site. Many of the site management tasks may seem boring, but they can make or break the success of your site.

You may not need to change the design that often, but you do want to add new content to your site at least that often. You can add new images, new text, new links, and so forth.

FLUID DYNAMICS

Web sites should be dynamic. That's the beauty of the Web. It is constantly changing and so should your Web site. Updating and changing your site should become a regular and routine activity. You should add pages or delete them as the need arises. Local and external links as well as images and multimedia files should all be checked and kept up to date to compliment any new content you add.

Links should lead visitors to destinations. Broken links only lead visitors down blind alleys or to dead ends. When this happens, your visitors lose respect for your site and confidence in your abilities.

A Web site that doesn't function as it should greatly affects the image you want to portray as well as your credibility. Even minor errors like spelling mistakes, affect your image. Images that can't be found, links that go nowhere, and forms that don't work can destroy your image. If you combine more than one of these problems on your site, you can say goodbye to your visitors.

QUICK 🔘 PAINLESS

Site management involves a broad range of skills. Many of these skills you learned as you built your site. The others are simple organization skills.

Many HTML editors offer a spell checker as part of the program. Use this to make sure you haven't made any typo or spelling errors in your pages. This is the easiest step to take to make sure your pages have as few errors as possible.

Next, set up a schedule to check your links on a regular basis. Set up a certain day each week or each month to check your links. If any are broken or the linked site is no longer there, delete them or replace them with new links. If you update pages in your site that are internally linked, make sure all those links still work correctly as well.

It's fairly easy to see if all your images work properly. If they're not, instead of the image, you get a broken image graphic. Generally this means the image file is missing. Later in this chapter we'll teach you how to troubleshoot for and fix this small problem.

One of the basic elements of site management is becoming familiar with your site's structure. Organizing the pages and files for your site is one important step in managing your site. Good organization helps you keep track of your links and guarantee against losing graphics. This also helps when you have to update your site. It's easier to find things when there's a logic to the chaos that sites can become.

If you have the time, you can perform all these activities yourself. However, if you have a really large site, this can be quite daunting and time consuming, especially if you have a lot of links and images. If time is an issue for you, as it is for most of us, there's hope.

YOU'LL THANK YOURSELF LATER

Use the Search and Replace option in your HTML editor to perform a global search of all the pages in your site to replace broken links.

IF YOU'RE SO
INCLINED

You can find more site management tools at these sites:

ZDnet Products—
www.zdnet.com/products/
sitemanagementtoolsuser.
html

Builder.com—www.builder.
com/ (select Builder
Downloads)

Simply perform a search for Web site management tools.

Fortunately for us there are wonderful people out there who either have the time or whose job it is to create software to make our jobs easier and save us all this valuable time. There are several programs that help you manage your site.

Some of the HTML editors even give you some features to help you in these tasks. One such feature is the search and replace option. This feature lets you search for keywords or links and replace them with other words or links. The editors also let you set your pages up in an organization that makes sense for you. As mentioned in previous chapters, keep all the files, images, and pages for your Web site together, preferably in the same program files. This makes it so much easier to upload to your Web address and it helps you when it comes time to update. Using a consistent and logical file naming system also helps you keep track of your files and know at a glance where each file belongs on your site.

If you'd rather not spend the time yourself checking all your links and images or if your site is just so big it would take you hours if not days, there are several programs you can get to help you manage your site. Be aware most of these programs are pretty pricey. But they can be well worth their weight in gold if they save you time and keep your site in tip-top shape.

These Web diagnostic tools primarily check the validity of links on your site. They give you a way to see and select specific pages with problem links. They also display the geography of your site in a way that gives you a clear view of any problems. They provide a total picture of your site so you can locate and fix any problems.

Following are some of these Web diagnostic programs available:

- BMC Software's Patrol—www.bmc.com

- Astra SiteManager—www.mere-int.com

- Optimal Application Insight—www.optimal.com

- WebWatcher Java Edition—www.caravelle.com

- BiggByte Software's InfoLink Link Checker— www.biggbyte.com

- TetraNet Software's LinkBot Pro— www.tetranetsoftware.com

Which one you choose is entirely up to you. Base your decision on the features you need and the amount of money you're willing to spend.

START ME UP

Once you have your site built and hung, you need to make sure it's accessible to everyone. You especially want to make sure it's viewable from the major browsers.

The two major browsers are Microsoft Internet Explorer and Netscape Navigator. Another major player is the Lynx browser. This is a text-only browser. There are dozens of other browsers available, these are just the major ones.

If you don't have copies of all of these browsers you need to get copies. Then you need to test your site on all of them. Open each browser and enter your address.

IF YOU'RE SO INCLINED

You can find various browsers at these software sites:

Tucows—www.tucows.com

Strouds—cws.internet.com/

Simply access the browser sections of these sites and choose the browsers you want to download.

When your site comes up, test all the pages to make sure all the links work and all the images show up as they should. If you detect any problems, fix them. Sometimes it's just a matter of altering the code a little.

A ROOM OF MY OWN

In a previous chapter we discussed server space for your site. Most ISPs give you a certain amount of space as part of their service package. Generally this is between 2 and 5 megabytes of space.

Most ISPs don't designate how you can use that. They just deduct any space that you use on their service from this figure. You can use it all for your Web site, or you can use it for FTP space also. If you have large archive files you want to offer to others so they can upload some of your files, this is the ideal way to do it.

Generally 2-5 MB of server space is sufficient for a typical Web site. However, if you have a large site or one with a lot of graphics, this might not be enough. In that case you need to negotiate for more space. All ISPs and Web site service companies are willing to give you more space for a fee.

Simply call or email them for a quote. They'll need to know how much more space you need. They may also want to know the purpose of your site. If it's a business site, they may charge you an additional fee for the amount of usage your site generates.

The way in which Web services and ISPs charge the fees for Web space is as varied as the services. You'll just have to call and ask questions. Then decide how you want to handle the increase in expense.

TROUBLE COMES TO TOWN

As much as we'd like it to be, we just don't live in a perfect world. Almost daily we deal with one problem or another. The world of the Web is no different.

From time to time, you're going to experience problems with your site. You may even start off with a problem. However, very few, if any, of these problems are life threatening to your site. That is, if you attack them immediately and don't let them become ongoing problems.

One of the first problems you might encounter is when you first upload your site to your Web address. After you upload it and go to your address to check it, you might notice your page isn't there. All that's there is an index page listing all the pages and graphics for your site.

This is an easy problem to fix. What has happened is that the Web server isn't recognizing the file name. All you have to do is rename your main page. The main page should be called index.htm or index.html. After you rename the file, upload it again and check to make sure that's fixed the problem.

Another problem you might encounter is a broken image. You'll know you have a broken image if a broken graphic shows up in place of the image you know should be there. When this happens it generally means the server can't find the image. This is very easy to fix. Just make sure the image is uploaded with your Web pages. If it's not, use your FTP client to upload it.

QUICK ▧ PAINLESS

A quick check of your site on a regular basis such as daily or weekly helps you detect and correct problems quickly and preserve your site's integrity.

If your image is loaded, then you need to check your source code. Make sure the code identifies the correct filename and path. A mistype in the address can cause this problem also.

Broken links aren't so easy to detect. About the only way you're going to know if a link isn't working is to test it. Click on the link. If it doesn't lead to the destination it's supposed to, or the destination is dead, you'll have to delete that link or alter it for another location.

From time to time you might get notice from visitors or you might notice yourself, that you can't access your site at all. You get a 404 URL Not Found error or something similar. Generally this has something to do with your Web provider. But just to make sure, check your site through your FTP client to make sure that all your files are uploaded. If they are, a simple call to your provider should give you answers to when they anticipate the problem should be resolved and your site back online. There's nothing you can do if it's your provider's problem but be patient.

If your provider exhibits a pattern of excessive downtime, then you should consider finding a new provider. Excessive downtime would involve being down more than a day or being down several times a month or more.

Because the Internet relies on phone lines, satellites, and machines, downtime is inevitable. Construction companies cut phone lines, sunspots and debris in space affect satellites, and machines break down. However, when it becomes excessive, the provider either isn't taking care of their equipment, has inadequate technicians, or exhibits poor planning. In either case, it's time to look for a more reliable provider. If you're site is inaccessible too often, your visitors will cease to visit you. And if your site is there to promote your business, it will cost you money each time it's down.

These are the most common problems you'll run across with your site. This section should help you resolve them quickly and get your site back into shape.

Managing your site can be quite a chore, but a necessary evil. Keeping your site updated and changing the content from time to time helps keep your visitors returning to it. Chant after me: *Change is good. Change is our friend.*

Put on some rocking tunes and launch your favorite HTML editor. Use the guidelines in this book to create an awesome site. When you have it designed to your satisfaction, show it off to everyone you know. Then register it so that you can bring in people all over the globe. Keep it updated and you'll keep people coming back.

Make yourself a little plaque that says *I am a Web Master!* Be proud!

Part 5

More Lazy Stuff

How to Get Someone Else to Do It For You

If you'd rather not experience the satisfaction of building your own site, you can always get someone else to do it for you. You have two choices.

One choice is to use the neighbor's teenage or college son or daughter. These kids were raised using computers. They can almost whip a site together with their eyes closed.

Your second option is to hire someone to design and build your site. On just about any Web corner you can find a Web designing service. For a fee these services will not only create your pages, but most also scan photos, register your site with the search engines, and host your site on their Web server. Just about anything involved in creating Web pages, these services can and will do for you, if you're willing to pay for it.

The fees range from $50 for one simple, basic page to thousands of dollars for larger, more complex sites. Then there's additional charges for disk space on their servers, listing with search engines, and additional email addresses.

Even if you hire someone else or let the kid next door build your site, you still have to provide these people with the content for your site; tell them specifically what you want. You'll need to provide them with a basic idea of what you want, the photos or images, background information on you or your company, and so forth.

Some of the Web services charge a flat per page design rate then add separate charges for extras such as forms, catalogs, guestbooks, counters, logos, animation, scanning, and so forth. Some give you a flat rate quote according to how you want your site set up and how much work is involved.

Shop around. Check prices and references to find the Web service that's best for you and your needs. A simple search on any of the search engines gives you hundreds of Web services to choose from. You'll likely find several in your hometown.

You could also ask friends and family who they recommend. Or you could ask your ISP to refer you to someone. A reputable and reliable Web designer service is relatively easy to locate.

B

If You Really Want More, Read These

There are dozens of books available to assist you in building your Web site. There are also many sites on the Web to help. The ZDnet site at www.zdnet.com/ and the Builder.com site at www.builder.com both have numerous pages and articles filled with helpful information on techniques you can use to build a killer site.

Following is a list of books to help you. Included in this list are books about some of the areas that were too advanced to cover in this book.

- *Creating Killer Web Sites, Second Edition,* David S. Siegel (Hayden Books, 1997)

- *Creating Web Pages for Dummies, (3rd Ed),* Bud E. Smith, Arthur Bebak (IDG Books, 1998)

- *Creating Cool Html 4 Web Pages,* Dave Taylor (IDG Books, 1998)

- *CGI Primer Plus for Windows : Learn to Create Interactive Web Pages,* Mohammed J. Kabir (Waite Group Press, 1996)

- *Designing With JavaScript: Creating Dynamic Web Pages,* Nick Heinle (O'Reilly & Associates, 1997)

- *Javascript Primer Plus: Enhancing Web Pages With the Javascript Programming Language*, Gabriel Torok, Jeffrey Payne, Matt Weisfeld, Paul Tyma et al (Waite Group Press, 1996)

- *Web Design Resources Directory: Tools and Techniques for Designing Your Web Pages*, Ray Davis, Eileen Mullin (Macmillan Computer Publishing, 1997)

This list should get you started. A study of the titles your local bookstore carries will give you even more to select from.

If You Don't Know What It Means, Look Here

Alignment. Indicates how something should align with text or graphics.

Anchor. An HTML tag used to create links to other Web pages or sites.

Animated GIFS. Images with motion.

<BODY> HTML tag to designate the main part of an HTML document that's displayed on the Web.

Cell Padding. The amount of space between the contents of a cell and the border of a cell.

Cell Spacing. Indicates the amount of space to place in the cells of a table in a Web page.

Client. Another term for a computer program.

Definition List. A list of terms and their definitions.

Directory List. Used to display a list of file names.

Font. A particular use of a typeface. Arial is a typeface while Arial 10-point bold is a font.

<FORM>   An HTML command that enables site designers to input data in a variety of ways.

Frames.   Independent sections of a Web page or mini windows.

FTP   File Transfer Protocol is the way files are sent and received over the Internet.

GIF   Compuserve's Graphics Interchange Format, which is an image format.

Guestbook.   Form on a page that lets visitors send comments to the page designer or owner.

GUI   Graphical User Interface.

<HEAD>   Formatting code used to indicate a heading or subheading in a Web document.

Hex Codes.   Codes used to designate certain colors.

Hidden Comments.   Comments you insert into Web documents which don't appear in the viewed documents.

Hits.   Number of visitors that access a site.

Home Page.   The beginning document seen by visitors to your Web site. Also referred to as the Front Door.

Horizontal Rule.   A thick horizontal line through a Web page which creates vertical separation of parts of that page.

Hostname.   The combination of computer and domain names that describes a particular computer or user on the Internet, indicated with the <HR> code.

Hot Link.   An image or text you can click that leads to something else.

HTML   HyperText Markup Language which is the language that's used to define and describe the page layout of documents displayed on the Web.

HTML Editor. A program that assists you in creating Web pages, also referred to as Web page authoring programs.

HTML Tag. An information instruction within an HTML document.

HTTP HyperText Transfer Protocol is the procedure for collecting and displaying HTML documents.

Hyperlink. Text or graphic that is linked to another page or site on the Web.

Hypertext. An interconnected web of text information where a word or phrase links to another place in the document or to another document.

Image Map. A picture with different areas or regions that are mapped to different hyperlinks, where clicking on different areas produces different results.

ISP Internet Service Provider is the service you use to connect to the Internet.

JPEG Joint Photographic Experts Group and a graphics format.

Line Break. A line space inserted into an HTML document using the <BR> code.

Link. A word, graphic or other area of a Web page that visitors can click to move to another spot in the document or to another document.

Lynx. A text-only UNIX Web browser.

Mailto. The Internet protocol used for sending email via a Web browser.

Marquees. Scrolling text you can insert into Web pages.

Markup Language. A special type of programming language that lets users describe the desired appearance and structural features of a document.

Menu Lists.   List of items, usually choices, and limited to one item per line.

METAMeta Tags.   Keywords to describe your pages that don't appear in the viewed page but are seen by search engines.

Multimedia.   Any combination of text, graphics, audio, and video.

Navigation Bar.   Similar to a toolbar but in a Web page which helps visitors know where they can go and what they can do at your site.

Nested List.   A list within a list.

Nested Table.   A table within a table.

Ordered List.   A list of terms, often numbered, that describes steps in a process.

Paired Tags.   Set of tags used to designate format codes.

Pointer.   A word, graphic, or other area that users click to move to another area in the document or to another document; same as link.

Server.   A computer or computer program that provides information or services to other computers or computer programs.

Scripts.   Mini programs which perform specific activities.

Search Engine.   A tool that lets users or visitors search by keyword for specific information.

Source Code.   The code used to create a Web document.

<TABLE>   Formatting code that lets you create a table in your pages.

Thumbnail Image.   A small version of a larger image.

Tiled Images.   A background image created by altering a series of images.

Timestamps.   Update information included on Web pages.

<TITLE>   Formatting code used to designate the title for a Web document.

URL   Uniform Resource Locator which is the standard way that resources are identified by Web browsers.

Unordered List.   A list of terms that have no implied order, such as a bulleted list.

Unpaired Tags.   One tag that's used to designate a format code.

Wallpaper.   Texture used for backgrounds in Web pages.

Web.   Also known as the World Wide Web. It is a service on the Internet that lets users display multimedia documents.

Web Browser.   A program that lets you view Web pages on the Internet.

Web Page.   A document created using HTML that is displayed on the Web.

Web Site.   A collection of Web pages.

D

It's Time for Your Reward

Wow! Can you believe it?! You did it! You built your site! And what a fantastic job you did. You should reward yourself. You deserve it. Plan a night on the town. Take yourself and a significant other to your favorite restaurant. Then see a show or go to a concert. To top the evening off, book a room in a nice motel or hotel. End the night with a glass of champagne and chocolate covered strawberries. Toast the success your site is sure to be! And toast yourself for making it all happen!

Index

maintenance, Web page
design, 38
managing
Web pages, 49
Web sites, HTML
(Hypertext Markup
Language) editors, 246
manipulating graphics
HTML (Hypertext Markup
Language) editors,
166, 168
loading faster, 162-163
Site Builder, 168-169,
171-172
size, 158-160
text, loading, 161-162
thumbnails, 164-166
transparencies, 163-164
marquees
commands, 191-192
home page usage, 190
scrolling, 191
Matt's Script Archive
Web site, 96
MCI Web site, 37
menu lists, 117
Meta tags, 187-188
search engines, 236, 238
metajacking, 237
Method tag, 176
Mickey's Collection
Web site, 192
Microsoft Internet Explorer,
see Internet Explorer
MIDI Farm Web site, 208
Midi files Web site, 62
Mosaic, 7
MPEG (Motion Picture
Experts Group), 210
multimedia, 7

N

Name command, 196
naming conventions,
graphic files, 162-163
navigation
graphical, 7

headers, 54
Web pages, organizing,
51-54
Web sites, designing, 78-79
navigation bar, 80
nested lists, 118
nested tables, 92, 134, 136
Netscape
Communicator, 14
Netscape's What's New
Page Web site, 225
Netsurfer Focus
Web site, 65
Noframe command, 204
Non-Dithering Colors
Web site, 99
Nospam, 228
Numbered List icon, 118

OB Home Net
Web site, 223
1-4-All, 11, 27
creating lists, 120-122,
124-125
designing Web pages,
105, 107-109
Insert Image dialog
box, 167
Online Medical
Dictionary, 78
Open Market
Web site, 225
ordered lists
creating, 119
tags, 115
organization, 51-54
resources links, 56

P

pages, see Web pages
paired HTML (Hypertext
Markup Language)
tags, 23-25
paired tags, anchors, 174
Paragraph Break tag, 25
Paragraph tag, 154

PDF (Portable Document
Format) files, 66-67
performance indicators,
238-241
forms, 38
hit counters, 38
Web pages, 227
Pete's TV WAVs
Web site, 208
pictures, see graphics
pop-up box forms, 196
Portable Document Format
files (PDF), 66-67
PPP (Point-to-Point
Protocol), 15, 18
problem solving, updating
Web pages, 249-251
Product Web site, 225
protocols
FTP (File Transfer
Protocol), 218-219, 221
HTTP (Hypertext Transfer
Protocol), 7
PPP (Point-to-Point
Protocol), 18
SLIP (Serial Line Internet
Protocol), 17

Quick Time video
format, 210

radio button forms, 196
real-time report access traffic analysis tool, 240
reference links, 55
Register It Web site, 224
registering Web sites
with search engines,
223-224
with services, 223-224
related resources links, 55
researching Web sites, 88
Reset button, 198
robots, keywords, 236
Row Span tag, 137-138

Rows command, 203